# The Republican Agenda: Undoing 200 Years of Democracy for a Dictatorship

Adrian Rocquecliffe

Published by Writers Sidekick Publishing, 2024.

While every precaution has been taken in the preparation of this book, the publisher assumes no responsibility for errors or omissions, or for damages resulting from the use of the information contained herein.

THE REPUBLICAN AGENDA: UNDOING 200 YEARS OF DEMOCRACY FOR A DICTATORSHIP

**First edition. August 31, 2024.**



ISBN: 979-8227237101

Written by Adrian Rocquecliffe.

# Table of Contents

# Part I - Undoing 200 Years of Democracy for a Dictatorship

The book "The Republican Agenda: Undoing 200 Years of Democracy for a Dictatorship" argues that the Republican Party's actions are eroding the democratic foundations of the United States. The central thesis suggests that the party's current trajectory is steering the country away from democracy and towards a dictatorship, challenging the principles that have guided the nation for over two centuries.

# The Central Thesis:

In "The Republican Agenda: Undoing 200 Years of Democracy for a Dictatorship," the central thesis posits that the current direction of the Republican Party is actively undermining the democratic principles upon which the United States was founded. This shift is not just a series of isolated political maneuvers but a coordinated effort to erode the foundations of democracy and replace them with a more authoritarian, dictatorial model of governance. This transformation poses significant risks not only to the nation as a whole but also to groups that may initially seem insulated from such changes, specifically Privileged White Americans.

## *Erosion of Democratic Institutions*

The Republican agenda involves a systematic weakening of key democratic institutions that safeguard the balance of power in the U.S. government. Through tactics like voter suppression, gerrymandering, and efforts to discredit and dismantle the free press, the party is effectively eroding the mechanisms that ensure accountability and representation. By undermining the electoral process and the judiciary, the party seeks to entrench its power, limiting the ability of the electorate to challenge or change leadership through democratic means.

Privileged White Americans, who may currently enjoy a strong influence over these institutions due to their socio-economic status, could find that their control diminishes as power becomes increasingly centralized in the hands of a few. The loss of a functional democracy means that even those who once had a voice in shaping the nation's direction may find themselves marginalized if they are not part of the ruling elite.

## *Centralization of Power and the Rise of Authoritarianism*

The agenda also involves a deliberate concentration of power within the executive branch, reducing the checks and balances that are essential in a democratic system. The erosion of Congress's power and the weakening of judicial independence allows for the rise of authoritarian leadership, where decisions are made unilaterally and without the input or consent of the governed.

For Privileged White Americans, this centralization of power could initially seem beneficial, as they might assume that their interests will be protected by a government that aligns with their views. However, as the government becomes more authoritarian, the protection of their rights and privileges becomes increasingly dependent on their loyalty to the regime. Any deviation from the party line could lead to a loss of status, influence, or even personal freedoms.

## Suppression of Dissent and Opposition

A critical component of the Republican agenda is the suppression of dissent, both within the party and in society at large. This involves targeting political opponents, controlling the media narrative, and using legal means to stifle protests and silence critics. In an authoritarian system, dissent is not tolerated, and those who oppose the ruling party can face severe consequences.

Privileged White Americans, who might initially feel secure under a regime that aligns with their values, could find themselves vulnerable if they ever fall out of favor with those in power. The suppression of dissent doesn't discriminate based on prior status or privilege; those who challenge the regime could be subjected to the same repressive measures as anyone else. Over time, the ability to express differing opinions, engage in free debate, or advocate for change could be severely curtailed, leading to an oppressive environment where conformity is enforced.

## Manipulation of Public Perception and the Role of Propaganda

The Republican agenda includes a concerted effort to control the narrative through the use of propaganda and misinformation. By manipulating public perception, the party seeks to maintain its hold on power by fostering divisions, creating scapegoats, and promoting a narrow, controlled worldview. This manipulation is intended to keep the public in line and prevent any significant challenge to the authority of the ruling party.

Privileged White Americans might find themselves caught in a web of misinformation, where their understanding of the world is shaped by the regime's agenda. This could lead to a narrowing of perspectives, where dissenting voices are drowned out, and critical thinking is discouraged. While they may initially benefit from a system that supports their worldview, the long-term effects could include a loss of intellectual freedom and a decrease in the quality of information available to them.

## Undermining the Electoral Process

A cornerstone of democratic governance is the integrity of the electoral process, which ensures that leaders are chosen by the people in free and fair elections. The Republican agenda's efforts to undermine this process through actions like discrediting election results, restricting voter access, and spreading misinformation are aimed at creating an environment where elections become mere formalities, with outcomes that are predetermined by those in power.

For Privileged White Americans, this could mean a future where their vote holds less significance and their ability to influence political outcomes is diminished. As elections lose their legitimacy, the government becomes less accountable to the people, including those who have traditionally held significant sway in political matters. The erosion of electoral integrity threatens the very foundation of their influence, leaving them increasingly powerless in a system that no longer reflects the will of the people.

## Impact on Privileged White Americans

While Privileged White Americans might initially perceive benefits from the Republican agenda, such as tax cuts, deregulation, and policies that align with their economic interests, the long-term impact could be profoundly negative. The move towards authoritarianism threatens the stability and predictability that many privileged individuals rely on for their continued success and influence.

As democratic institutions weaken, the rule of law becomes less consistent, and protections that once seemed guaranteed may be arbitrarily applied or disregarded entirely. Privileged individuals could find themselves vulnerable to the whims of an increasingly autocratic leadership, where their rights, wealth, and status are contingent on their loyalty to the regime.

Additionally, the social unrest and inequality that often accompany authoritarian regimes could lead to a more volatile society, where the divide between the privileged and the rest of the population becomes a source of tension and conflict. This instability could erode the quality of life for even the most privileged as they navigate a society where their position is no longer secure.

Moreover, the ethical and moral implications of supporting a regime that undermines democracy may weigh heavily on Privileged White Americans. As the country moves further away from its democratic ideals, it may face a reckoning with the legacy it leaves for future generations, a legacy defined by complicity in the erosion of freedoms and the rise of dictatorship.

## *In Essence*

The central argument of "The Republican Agenda: Undoing 200 Years of Democracy for a Dictatorship" is that the current Republican strategy is not just a political shift but a dangerous move towards authoritarianism that threatens the very fabric of American democracy. While Privileged White Americans might initially benefit from some aspects of this agenda, they are not immune to its long-term consequences. As democracy erodes and power becomes more concentrated, even those who have traditionally enjoyed privilege and influence may find themselves facing a future where their rights, freedoms, and way of life are at serious risk. The book serves as a critical warning about the perils of sacrificing democratic principles for short-term gains, emphasizing that in the march toward dictatorship, no one remains truly safe.

# Historical Context: A 200-Year Journey of American Democracy and Its Foundational Principles

The United States of America was founded on the principles of democracy, a system of government by the people for the people. Over the past 200 years, American democracy has evolved, shaped by pivotal moments in history, landmark legal decisions, and the enduring commitment to the ideals of liberty, equality, and justice. To understand the current threats posed by the Republican agenda, it's essential first to explore the historical context of American democracy and the foundational principles that have guided the nation since its inception.

## *The Birth of American Democracy: The Founding Fathers and the Constitution*

The roots of American democracy can be traced back to the late 18th century when the Founding Fathers declared independence from British rule and sought to create a new government based on the principles of popular sovereignty, individual rights, and the separation of powers. The drafting of the U.S. Constitution in 1787 was a groundbreaking moment in history, as it established a framework for governance that balanced power between the executive, legislative, and judicial branches.

The Constitution also embedded key democratic principles, such as the rule of law, checks and balances, and the protection of civil liberties. The Bill of Rights, added in 1791, further ensured that individual freedoms, such as freedom of speech, religion, and assembly, were protected from government overreach. These foundational documents and the principles they enshrined set the stage for the development of a democratic society where power is derived from the consent of the governed.

## *The Expansion of Democracy: The Struggle for Voting Rights*

In the early years of the republic, the right to vote was limited to a small segment of the population, primarily white male property owners. However, over the next two centuries, American democracy expanded as various groups fought for and won the right to participate in the electoral process. The 15th Amendment (1870) granted African American men the right to vote, and the 19th Amendment (1920) extended suffrage to women.

The Civil Rights Movement of the 1960s was another pivotal period in the expansion of democracy. The Voting Rights Act of 1965 addressed racial discrimination in voting, ensuring that all citizens, regardless of race, had equal access to the ballot box. These struggles and victories were essential in making the United States a more inclusive democracy where the voices of all citizens could be heard and represented.

## The Role of Institutions: Checks and Balances in a Democratic System

One of the key features of American democracy is the system of checks and balances, designed to prevent any one branch of government from becoming too powerful. This system was implemented to safeguard against tyranny and ensure that the government remains accountable to the people. The executive, legislative, and judicial branches each have distinct powers, with mechanisms in place to check and balance each other's authority.

Over the past 200 years, this system has been tested through numerous crises, including wars, political scandals, and economic downturns. Despite these challenges, the checks and balances embedded in the U.S. Constitution have generally functioned as intended, preventing the concentration of power and preserving the democratic process.

## The Evolution of Political Parties: From Unity to Polarization

Political parties have played a significant role in shaping American democracy. Initially, the Founding Fathers were wary of factions, fearing they would divide the nation. However, political parties soon emerged as essential components of the democratic process, providing a platform for debate and competition in elections.

Over time, the American political landscape has become increasingly polarized, particularly in recent decades. The rise of extreme partisanship has led to gridlock in government and a growing divide among the electorate. This polarization has strained the democratic process, making it more challenging to find common ground and address the needs of the nation as a whole.

## *The Defense of Democracy: Key Moments in Preserving Democratic Ideals*

Throughout its history, American democracy has faced numerous threats, both internal and external. The Civil War (1861-1865) was a defining moment when the nation fought to preserve the Union and the principle that all people are created equal. Similarly, the New Deal era (1933-1939) saw significant government intervention to address the Great Depression, reinforcing the idea that democracy must also address economic inequality and provide for the common good.

The Cold War (1947-1991) further solidified the United States' commitment to democracy, as the nation positioned itself as a global leader in the fight against totalitarianism. The fall of communism and the spread of democratic ideals worldwide were seen as victories for the American democratic model, reinforcing the belief in the superiority of democratic governance.

## *Challenges to Democracy: The Modern Era*

In the modern era, American democracy faces new challenges, including the rise of misinformation, the influence of money in politics, and increasing political polarization. The concentration of power in the hands of a few, coupled with efforts to undermine the integrity of elections, poses a serious threat to the democratic process.

The Republican agenda, as discussed in this book, represents one of the most significant challenges to American democracy in recent history. By undermining democratic institutions and promoting authoritarian tendencies, this agenda threatens to undo the progress made over the past 200 years and replace a government of the people with a government that serves only the interests of a select few.

### *Impact on Privileged White Americans: A Historical Perspective*

Historically, Privileged White Americans have often been the primary beneficiaries of the nation's democratic system, enjoying economic, social, and political advantages. However, the move towards authoritarianism, as seen in the current Republican agenda, threatens to upend this status quo.

In previous eras, when democracy was under threat, privileged groups often believed they were insulated from the consequences. Yet history shows that the erosion of democratic principles ultimately leads to instability, conflict, and a loss of rights for all citizens, including those who initially supported or benefited from the shift in power. The lessons of history underscore the fact that the preservation of democracy is in the best interest of all citizens, regardless of their status or privilege.

In Essence The 200-year history of American democracy is a testament to the resilience of the nation's foundational principles of liberty, equality, and justice. However, these principles are not guaranteed; they must be continually defended against threats from within and outside the government. The current Republican agenda, as it undermines these democratic ideals, poses a grave risk not only to the nation as a whole but also to the very groups that may initially seem to benefit from such a shift. Understanding the historical context of American democracy highlights the importance of vigilance in preserving the freedoms and rights that define the United States.

## Purpose of the Book: Examining the Threats to Democracy Posed by the Republican Agenda

The purpose of "The Republican Agenda: Undoing 200 Years of Democracy for a Dictatorship" is to provide a comprehensive examination of the actions, policies, and strategies of the contemporary Republican Party that are seen as direct threats to the foundational principles of American democracy. This book seeks to not only highlight these concerning trends but also to offer an analysis of their potential consequences for the future of the United States. By bringing these issues to the forefront, the book aims to inform, engage, and ultimately mobilize readers to recognize the dangers posed by the current trajectory of the Republican Party.

## *Unmasking the Agenda: Identifying Authoritarian Tendencies*

The first goal of the book is to unmask the underlying agenda of the Republican Party as it moves away from traditional democratic values and toward a more authoritarian model of governance. This includes a detailed exploration of the policies and strategies that reflect these authoritarian tendencies, such as the erosion of voting rights, the undermining of judicial independence, and the increasing centralization of power in the executive branch.

By systematically dissecting these actions, the book aims to reveal how they collectively contribute to a broader agenda that threatens to dismantle the democratic institutions that have defined the United States for over two centuries. The intent is to make clear that these are not isolated incidents but part of a deliberate strategy to consolidate power and limit the checks and balances that prevent autocracy.

## *Analyzing Policies: How Specific Policies Threaten Democracy*

Another key purpose of the book is to analyze specific policies implemented or advocated by the Republican Party that have the potential to weaken democratic norms and institutions. These include measures like voter suppression laws, gerrymandering, efforts to undermine the independence of the judiciary, and the spread of misinformation. Each policy is examined in terms of its immediate impact on the democratic process and its long-term implications for the health of American democracy.

The book seeks to provide readers with a clear understanding of how these policies erode the democratic principles of fairness, accountability, and equal representation. By breaking down complex issues into accessible explanations, the book aims to equip readers with the knowledge they need to evaluate the policies being implemented by their leaders critically.

## *Exposing Strategies: The Manipulation of Public Opinion*

The book also focuses on exposing the strategies used by the Republican Party to manipulate public opinion and maintain support for its agenda. This includes the use of propaganda, misinformation, and fear-mongering to sway public perception and distract from the erosion of democratic norms. The book delves into how these tactics are employed to create a narrative that justifies the concentration of power and the marginalization of dissenting voices.

By examining these strategies, the book aims to raise awareness about the ways in which public opinion is being shaped to support an agenda that ultimately undermines democracy. The goal is to encourage readers to question the information they receive, seek out diverse perspectives, and resist being manipulated by partisan rhetoric.

### *Exploring the Impact: Consequences for American Society*

A critical aspect of the book's purpose is to explore the broader impact of the Republican agenda on American society as a whole, including its effects on various demographic groups. The book discusses how the erosion of democracy disproportionately affects marginalized communities while also addressing the potential consequences for privileged groups, such as Privileged White Americans, who may initially support the agenda.

The book seeks to illustrate that the threats to democracy posed by the Republican agenda are not abstract concerns but have real and tangible effects on the lives of everyday Americans. By connecting the dots between policy decisions and their impact on the ground, the book aims to demonstrate the far-reaching consequences of undermining democratic principles.

### *Raising Awareness: Mobilizing Public Action*

One of the primary goals of the book is to raise awareness about the dangers of the current Republican agenda and to mobilize public action to defend democracy. The book calls on readers to recognize the urgency of the situation and to take an active role in protecting the democratic values that have been central to the American identity.

Through its analysis, the book aims to inspire readers to become more engaged in the political process, whether by voting, advocating for policy changes, participating in protests, or holding their representatives accountable. The book emphasizes that democracy is not a given; the people must actively defend it.

## *Offering Solutions: How to Protect Democracy*

Finally, the book seeks to offer solutions and strategies for protecting and revitalizing American democracy in the face of the threats posed by the Republican agenda. This includes recommendations for policy reforms, ways to strengthen democratic institutions and ideas for fostering greater civic engagement among the populace.

The purpose here is not only to critique the current state of affairs but also to provide a roadmap for how the country can move forward in a way that preserves the core principles of democracy. The book aims to empower readers with practical steps they can take to ensure that the United States remains a government of the people, by the people, and for the people.

In Essence The purpose of "The Republican Agenda: Undoing 200 Years of Democracy for a Dictatorship" is to offer a comprehensive examination of the ways in which the contemporary Republican Party is threatening the foundational principles of American democracy. By analyzing the actions, policies, and strategies that contribute to this erosion, the book aims to inform readers of the gravity of the situation and to inspire them to take action in defense of democratic values. Ultimately, the book seeks to serve as both a warning and a call to arms, reminding readers that the preservation of democracy is a collective responsibility that requires vigilance, awareness, and active participation.

# Chapter 1: The Roots of Republican Ideology

## Historical Background: Exploring the Origins and Initial Principles of the Republican Party

The Republican Party, one of the two major political parties in the United States, has a rich history that dates back to the mid-19th century. Formed in response to the nation's growing divisions over issues such as slavery, states' rights, and the expansion of the Union, the Republican Party was initially rooted in principles that emphasized freedom, equality, and national unity. It's essential to explore the origins of the Republican Party and the principles that guided its early leaders to understand how the party's current agenda deviates from its original mission,

### *The Birth of the Republican Party: A Response to National Crisis*

The Republican Party was founded in the 1850s amid a turbulent period in American history. The nation was deeply divided over the issue of slavery, particularly its expansion into new territories and states. The Kansas-Nebraska Act of 1854, which allowed these territories to decide for themselves whether to permit slavery, ignited fierce opposition among anti-slavery activists and politicians. This opposition led to the formation of a new political party, the Republican Party.

The party was established by a coalition of former Whigs, Free Soilers, anti-slavery Democrats, and abolitionists who shared a common goal: to prevent the spread of slavery into the western territories and to promote the idea of a free labor economy. The first official meeting of the Republican Party took place in Ripon, Wisconsin, in 1854, marking the beginning of what would become a powerful political force in American history.

### *The Foundational Principles: Liberty, Equality, and Union*

At its inception, the Republican Party was guided by several key principles that reflected the ideals of the time. Central to the party's platform was the belief in liberty and equality for all individuals, particularly the opposition to the institution of slavery. The early Republicans saw slavery as morally wrong and as a threat to the nation's democratic values. They believed that the expansion of slavery into new territories would undermine the principles of free labor and equality that were essential to the nation's economic and social progress.

Another foundational principle of the Republican Party was the preservation of the Union. The party's leaders were committed to maintaining the integrity of the United States and preventing the secession of Southern states, which threatened to tear the nation apart. This commitment to national unity would later become a defining feature of the Republican Party during the Civil War and the Reconstruction era that followed.

## *The Election of Abraham Lincoln: A Turning Point in American History*

The election of Abraham Lincoln as the 16th President of the United States in 1860 marked a turning point for the Republican Party and the nation as a whole. Lincoln's victory was a triumph for the anti-slavery movement. It solidified the Republican Party's position as the leading political force in the country. His election, however, also triggered the secession of Southern states, leading to the outbreak of the Civil War.

Under Lincoln's leadership, the Republican Party became synonymous with the fight to preserve the Union and end slavery. The Emancipation Proclamation of 1863, which declared the freedom of all enslaved people in Confederate-held territory, was a landmark achievement that reflected the party's commitment to human rights and equality. Lincoln's assassination in 1865, shortly after the end of the Civil War, further cemented his legacy as a symbol of the Republican Party's early principles.

## *Reconstruction and the Fight for Civil Rights*

Following the Civil War, the Republican Party played a crucial role in the Reconstruction era, a period of rebuilding the South and integrating formerly enslaved people into American society. The party's leaders championed the passage of the 13th, 14th, and 15th Amendments to the Constitution, which abolished slavery, granted citizenship to all persons born or naturalized in the United States, and protected the right to vote regardless of race, respectively.

During this period, the Republican Party was also instrumental in establishing civil rights protections for African Americans, including the creation of the Freedmen's Bureau, which assisted newly freed slaves. The party's commitment to civil rights and equality was evident in its efforts to rebuild the South on the basis of free labor, education, and equal protection under the law.

## *The Shift Toward Economic Policy: The Gilded Age and Industrialization*

As the nation moved into the late 19th century, the Republican Party began to shift its focus toward economic policy, particularly in response to the rapid industrialization and expansion of the American economy. The party increasingly aligned itself with business interests, advocating for tariffs to protect American industry, supporting the expansion of the railroads, and promoting policies that favored economic growth and innovation.

This period, known as the Gilded Age, saw the Republican Party become the party of big business and economic progress. While the party continued to support the principles of liberty and national unity, its emphasis on economic issues reflected the changing priorities of the nation as it transitioned from a primarily agricultural society to an industrial powerhouse.

## *The Evolution of Republican Principles: From Progressivism to Conservatism*

In the early 20th century, the Republican Party experienced a period of internal conflict and transformation. The Progressive Movement, which emerged within the party, sought to address the social and economic inequalities that had arisen during the Gilded Age. Leaders like Theodore Roosevelt advocated for reforms such as trust-busting, labor rights, and environmental conservation, which challenged the dominance of corporate interests within the party.

However, by the mid-20th century, the Republican Party began to shift away from its progressive roots and toward a more conservative ideology. A growing emphasis on limited government, free-market capitalism, and individual responsibility drove this shift. The party's support for civil rights waned. It began to attract voters who were opposed to the social changes of the 1960s, particularly in the South, where the party capitalized on resistance to desegregation and the Civil Rights Movement.

## *The Modern Republican Party: Continuity and Change*

In the latter half of the 20th century and into the 21st century, the Republican Party has continued to evolve, balancing its historical principles with the demands of modern politics. The party has maintained its commitment to limited government and economic conservatism while also embracing social conservatism, particularly on issues such as abortion, gun rights, and immigration.

At the same time, the Republican Party has faced criticism for moving away from its original principles of equality and national unity. The party's embrace of populist rhetoric, its stance on voting rights, and its challenges to the legitimacy of democratic institutions have sparked concerns that the Republican Party is straying from the values that defined its early years.

In Essence The Republican Party's origins are deeply rooted in the principles of liberty, equality, and national unity. From its founding in the 1850s through its role in the Civil War and Reconstruction, the party championed the fight against slavery and the preservation of the Union. However, as the party evolved, its focus shifted toward economic conservatism and limited government, leading to the modern Republican Party we see today. By understanding the historical background and initial principles of the Republican Party, readers can better grasp how the party's current actions and policies contrast with its founding ideals and why this shift poses a threat to the democratic principles that have guided the United States for over two centuries.

## Shift in Ideology: The Evolution of the Republican Party Over Time

The Republican Party, founded in the mid-19th century, has undergone significant ideological shifts throughout its history. Initially rooted in principles of anti-slavery, national unity, and economic modernization, the party has evolved in response to changing political, social, and economic landscapes. In recent decades, the Republican Party's ideology has shifted dramatically, reflecting a move away from its original progressive roots toward a more conservative and, in some cases, populist stance. This shift has redefined the party's identity and has had profound implications for American politics and society.

## The Early Republican Ideals: Anti-Slavery and National Unity

The Republican Party was founded in the 1850s as a coalition of anti-slavery activists, former Whigs, and abolitionists. Its early ideology was centered on the abolition of slavery, the promotion of free labor, and the preservation of the Union. These principles were encapsulated in the leadership of figures like Abraham Lincoln, who led the nation through the Civil War and worked to end slavery with the Emancipation Proclamation.

The party's commitment to equality and national unity continued into the Reconstruction era, with efforts to secure civil rights for newly freed African Americans and to rebuild the Southern states on the basis of free labor and equal protection under the law.

## The Gilded Age and the Rise of Economic Conservatism

As the United States entered the Gilded Age in the late 19th century, the Republican Party began to shift its focus toward economic policy. The party increasingly aligned itself with big business and industrial interests, advocating for high tariffs, infrastructure development, and the expansion of the railroad network. Economic conservatism became a defining feature of the party's platform, emphasizing the importance of a free-market economy, limited government intervention, and the protection of American industry.

This period marked the beginning of the party's association with the economic elite. This trend would continue to influence its policies and ideology in the decades to come. While the party maintained its support for civil rights during

Reconstruction, its focus on economic issues began to overshadow its earlier commitments to social equality.

## *The Progressive Era: A Temporary Shift Toward Reform*

In the early 20th century, the Republican Party experienced a temporary shift toward progressivism, driven by leaders like Theodore Roosevelt. The Progressive Movement within the party sought to address the social and economic inequalities that had emerged during the Gilded Age. This era saw the Republican Party championing reforms such as trust-busting, labor rights, environmental conservation, and government regulation of business to curb corporate power and protect consumers.

However, this progressive phase was short-lived, as internal divisions within the party led to a split between the progressive and conservative wings. By the 1920s, the Republican Party had largely returned to its conservative roots, focusing on limited government and free-market principles, while the progressive wing lost influence.

## *The New Deal and the Realignment of Party Ideologies*

The Great Depression and the subsequent New Deal era under President Franklin D. Roosevelt marked a significant realignment in American politics. The Democratic Party, which had traditionally been associated with states' rights and conservatism, embraced a more liberal agenda focused on government intervention to address economic inequality and social welfare. In response, the Republican Party positioned itself as the party of opposition to the New Deal, advocating for limited government, fiscal conservatism, and individual responsibility.

This period saw the Republican Party solidify its identity as the party of economic conservatism, opposing the expansion of federal government programs and regulations. The party's emphasis on free-market solutions and opposition to government intervention in the economy became central to its ideology, setting the stage for its modern conservative platform.

## *The Civil Rights Movement and the Southern Strategy*

The 1960s brought another significant ideological shift within the Republican Party, largely in response to the Civil Rights Movement. As the Democratic Party, particularly under President Lyndon B. Johnson, began to champion civil rights legislation, the Republican Party faced a choice: to support these efforts or to appeal to the growing discontent among white voters in the South who opposed desegregation and civil rights reforms.

The Republican Party's decision to adopt the "Southern Strategy" marked a turning point in its ideology. By appealing to the racial anxieties and conservative values of white Southern voters, the party shifted its base from the Northeast and Midwest to the South and West. This strategy not only changed the party's geographic stronghold but also led to an ideological shift toward social conservatism, particularly on issues related to race, states' rights, and law and order.

## *The Reagan Revolution: The Rise of Modern Conservatism*

The election of Ronald Reagan in 1980 marked the ascendancy of modern conservatism within the Republican Party. Reagan's presidency solidified the party's commitment to a conservative agenda that emphasized limited government, tax cuts, deregulation, and a strong national defense. Reagan's rhetoric of reducing the size of government and promoting individual freedom resonated with a broad coalition of voters, including religious conservatives, free-market advocates, and anti-communist hawks.

The Reagan era also saw the Republican Party embrace social conservatism, particularly in opposition to abortion, the Equal Rights Amendment, and LGBTQ+ rights. The alignment with the Religious Right became a cornerstone of the party's platform, as conservative Christian groups became a powerful and influential force within the party.

## *The Rise of Populism and the Trump Era*

The most recent and dramatic shift in the Republican Party's ideology occurred with the rise of populism and the election of Donald Trump in 2016. Trump's campaign and presidency were characterized by a rejection of traditional Republican orthodoxy on issues like free trade, fiscal conservatism, and foreign policy. Instead, Trump embraced a populist agenda that focused on nationalism, immigration restriction, and skepticism of globalism.

Trump's rhetoric and policies appealed to a base of voters who felt disillusioned with the political establishment and left behind by globalization and economic changes. His emphasis on "America First," the rejection of international alliances, and the use of divisive and inflammatory language marked a departure from the party's historical emphasis on national unity and responsible governance.

The Trump era also saw the Republican Party become increasingly polarized, with a growing divide between establishment conservatives and populist insurgents. The party's embrace of Trumpism has led to concerns about its commitment to democratic norms, as evidenced by efforts to undermine the 2020 election results and restrict voting rights.

### *The Current Ideological Landscape: Conservatism, Populism, and Division*

Today, the Republican Party's ideology is a complex and often contradictory mix of traditional conservatism, populism, and nationalism. The party remains committed to core conservative principles like limited government, free markets, and a strong national defense. Still, populist appeals to nationalism, immigration restriction, and cultural conservatism increasingly overshadow these.

The party's internal divisions, particularly between establishment conservatives and the populist wing, have created a fractured and volatile political landscape. The influence of Trump and his supporters continues to shape the party's direction, with debates over issues like immigration, trade, and foreign policy reflecting the tensions between these competing factions.

This shift in ideology has had significant implications for American democracy, as the Republican Party's embrace of populism and nationalism has led to a more polarized and contentious political environment. The party's willingness to challenge democratic norms and institutions, particularly in the wake of the 2020 election, has raised concerns about the future of the Republican Party and its role in the American political system.

In Essence The Republican Party's ideology has undergone significant transformations over the past century and a half. From its origins as a party of anti-slavery and national unity to its modern identity as a conservative, populist force, the Republican Party has continually adapted to the changing political landscape. However, these shifts have also led to internal conflicts and external criticisms, particularly as the party's commitment to democratic principles has come under scrutiny in recent years. Understanding this ideological evolution is key to grasping the current challenges facing the Republican Party and its impact on American democracy.

## Rise of Authoritarian Tendencies: Key Moments and Figures Shaping the Republican Shift

In recent decades, the Republican Party has increasingly embraced authoritarian tendencies, marked by a shift away from democratic norms and toward policies that concentrate power, undermine checks and balances, and challenge the rule of law. This trend has been driven by key moments and figures who have influenced the party's trajectory, leading to concerns about the erosion of democratic principles in the United States. Understanding these pivotal events and personalities is crucial to comprehend how the Republican Party has moved toward a more authoritarian approach.

### *The Southern Strategy: Exploiting Racial Tensions for Political Gain*

The Southern Strategy, implemented by Republican strategists in the late 1960s and 1970s, marked an early turn toward authoritarian tendencies within the party. By appealing to the racial anxieties of white Southern voters, the Republican Party sought to exploit division and fear to gain political power. This strategy relied on dog-whistle politics and coded language that stoked racial tensions while undermining the civil rights progress of the era.

The Southern Strategy's success in reshaping the political landscape of the South laid the groundwork for the Republican Party's future use of division and fear as tools to consolidate power. By prioritizing electoral success over national unity and democratic ideals, the party began a gradual shift toward more authoritarian tactics.

## *The Reagan Revolution: Expanding Executive Power*

Ronald Reagan's presidency in the 1980s is often celebrated for its conservative revolution. Still, it also marked a significant expansion of executive power. Reagan's administration pushed the boundaries of executive authority, particularly in foreign policy, through actions like the Iran-Contra affair. In this covert operation, Reagan's administration circumvented Congress to fund Nicaraguan rebels, showcasing a willingness to bypass democratic processes to achieve political goals.

This expansion of executive power under Reagan set a precedent for future Republican administrations, where the concentration of power in the executive branch became more pronounced. While Reagan himself maintained a strong commitment to democratic norms, his administration's actions planted the seeds for a more authoritarian approach in the years to come.

## *The Post-9/11 Era: The War on Terror and Erosion of Civil Liberties*

The terrorist attacks of September 11, 2001, marked a turning point in American politics, leading to the implementation of policies that significantly expanded government power at the expense of civil liberties. Under President George W. Bush, the Republican Party championed the USA PATRIOT Act, which granted the government sweeping surveillance powers, including the ability to monitor communications and detain individuals without due process.

The Bush administration's approach to the War on Terror, including the use of torture, indefinite detention at Guantanamo Bay, and warrantless wiretapping, reflected a shift toward authoritarian practices. These policies were justified in the name of national security. Still, they raised serious concerns about the erosion of constitutional protections and the balance of power in government.

The post-9/11 era also saw the rise of a more militarized and secretive state, where executive power was further concentrated, and checks and balances were increasingly sidelined. This period marked a significant step toward authoritarianism within the Republican Party, as the urgency of the War on Terror was used to justify actions that undermined democratic norms.

### *The Tea Party Movement: Populism and the Delegitimization of Government*

The rise of the Tea Party movement in the late 2000s represented a populist surge within the Republican Party, fueled by anger over government spending, taxation, and the perceived overreach of federal authority. While the Tea Party began as a grassroots movement, it quickly became associated with a more aggressive and confrontational style of politics that rejected compromise and sought to delegitimize government institutions.

The Tea Party's rhetoric often framed the government as an enemy of the people, fostering a distrust of democratic processes and institutions. This movement also gave rise to politicians who were willing to challenge the established norms of governance, pushing the party further toward authoritarian tendencies by advocating for policies that concentrated power in the hands of a few while undermining the role of government in society.

### *The Trump Presidency: A Full Embrace of Authoritarianism*

Donald Trump's election in 2016 marked the most significant and overt shift toward authoritarianism in the Republican Party's history. Trump's presidency was characterized by an open disdain for democratic norms, the rule of law, and the checks and balances that define the American political system. Throughout his time in office, Trump regularly attacked the media, questioned the legitimacy of elections, and sought to undermine independent institutions like the judiciary and the intelligence community.

One of the most notable examples of Trump's authoritarian tendencies was his refusal to accept the results of the 2020 presidential election, leading to baseless claims of widespread voter fraud and attempts to overturn the election results. This culminated in the January 6, 2021, attack on the U.S. Capitol, where Trump supporters, incited by his rhetoric, stormed the building in an effort to prevent the certification of the election.

Trump's presidency also saw the use of executive orders to bypass Congress, the politicization of the Justice Department, and attempts to coerce foreign governments into investigating political rivals. These actions reflected a clear departure from democratic principles and a move toward a more authoritarian style of governance, where power is concentrated in the hands of a single leader who operates above the law.

## *The Aftermath of Trump: Continued Challenges to Democracy*

Even after Trump left office, the Republican Party continued to exhibit authoritarian tendencies, particularly in its efforts to restrict voting rights and alter election laws in ways that could undermine future democratic processes. Many Republican-controlled state legislatures passed laws that imposed new voting restrictions, citing unfounded claims of voter fraud as justification. These actions raised concerns about the party's commitment to free and fair elections, a cornerstone of democracy.

The influence of Trumpism within the Republican Party has persisted, with many elected officials and candidates continuing to embrace his authoritarian rhetoric and policies. The party's shift toward authoritarianism has led to internal divisions. Still, the dominance of this approach within the party remains strong, raising questions about the future of American democracy and the Republican Party's role in it.

In Essence The rise of authoritarian tendencies within the Republican Party is the result of a series of key moments and figures who have gradually moved the party away from its commitment to democratic principles. From the Southern Strategy and the expansion of executive power under Reagan to the post-9/ 11 erosion of civil liberties, the Tea Party's populism, and the full embrace of authoritarianism under Trump, these developments have reshaped the party's ideology and approach to governance. Understanding these shifts is crucial to recognizing the challenges facing American democracy today and the role that the Republican Party plays in this evolving political landscape.

# Chapter 2: Erosion of Democratic Institutions

# Attacks on the Electoral System: Undermining Free and Fair Elections

The integrity of the electoral system is the foundation of a functioning democracy. In recent years, however, there have been concerted efforts by the Republican Party to undermine free and fair elections. These attacks on the electoral system include tactics like voter suppression, gerrymandering, and election interference. These strategies not only threaten the democratic process but also raise concerns about the long-term health of American democracy.

## *Voter Suppression: Limiting Access to the Ballot Box*

Restrictive Voting Laws: Voter suppression tactics have been increasingly used by the Republican Party to limit access to the ballot box, particularly for marginalized communities. These tactics include the implementation of strict voter ID laws, which disproportionately affect minority, elderly, and low-income voters who may not have the required identification. Other measures have also been used to make voting more difficult. Such as reducing early voting periods, closing polling stations in minority communities, purging voter rolls,

Impact on Voter Turnout: These restrictive measures have a significant impact on voter turnout, particularly among groups that traditionally lean Democratic. By making it harder for these populations to vote, the Republican Party has sought to tilt the electoral balance in its favor, raising concerns about the fairness and inclusiveness of the electoral process.

Recent Examples: In the wake of the 2020 presidential election, many Republican-controlled state legislatures passed laws that further restricted voting access. For example, Georgia's controversial SB 202 law reduced the availability of absentee ballots, restricted the use of ballot drop boxes, and made it illegal to provide food or water to voters waiting in long lines. These measures were widely criticized as efforts to suppress the vote in a state that had seen record turnout in 2020.

## *Gerrymandering: Manipulating Electoral Boundaries for Political Gain*

Definition and Purpose: Gerrymandering refers to the practice of drawing electoral district boundaries in a way that favors one political party over another. This tactic allows the party in power to create "safe" districts where their candidates are almost guaranteed to win, thereby reducing competition and entrenching their control over the political landscape.

Partisan Gerrymandering: The Republican Party has been particularly aggressive in using gerrymandering to secure electoral advantages. By manipulating district boundaries, Republicans have been able to create districts that dilute the voting power of Democratic-leaning constituencies, particularly in urban areas, while maximizing the influence of rural and suburban voters who tend to support the GOP.

Effects on Representation: Gerrymandering undermines the principle of equal representation by distorting the electoral map. It can lead to situations where a party wins a majority of seats in a legislature or Congress, even if it receives fewer overall votes than the opposing party. This distortion erodes public confidence in the electoral system and diminishes the responsiveness of elected officials to their constituents.

Legal Challenges: While gerrymandering has been challenged in court, the Supreme Court has largely refrained from intervening in cases of partisan gerrymandering, leaving the practice largely unchecked. This has allowed the party in power in many states, particularly Republicans, to continue drawing district lines to their advantage.

### *Election Interference: Undermining Trust in the Electoral Process*

False Claims of Voter Fraud: One of the most concerning developments in recent years has been the proliferation of false claims about widespread voter fraud, particularly following the 2020 presidential election. These baseless allegations, often promoted by prominent Republican figures, have been used to justify restrictive voting laws and efforts to overturn legitimate election results.

Impact on Public Trust: The repeated claims of voter fraud have had a corrosive effect on public trust in the electoral process. Polls have shown that a significant portion of Republican voters believe that the 2020 election was stolen despite a lack of evidence to support these claims. This erosion of trust poses a serious threat to the stability of the democratic system, as it fuels distrust and division among the electorate.

Attempts to Overturn Election Results: Perhaps the most dramatic example of election interference was the effort to overturn the results of the 2020 presidential election. After losing the election, President Donald Trump and his allies launched numerous legal challenges, all of which were unsuccessful. They pressured state officials to "find" votes to change the outcome. This culminated in the January 6, 2021, attack on the U.S. Capitol, where a mob, incited by Trump's rhetoric, attempted to prevent the certification of the election results.

Ongoing Threats: The push to undermine election results did not end with the 2020 election. Efforts to install partisan actors in key election oversight positions, as well as the continued spread of disinformation about election integrity, suggest that the threat of election interference remains a significant concern for future elections.

In Essence The attacks on the electoral system through voter suppression, gerrymandering, and election interference represent a concerted effort to undermine the principles of free and fair elections in the United States. These tactics, primarily employed by the Republican Party, not only threaten the integrity of the democratic process but also erode public trust in the system. As these challenges continue to evolve, the future of American democracy may depend on the ability to protect and strengthen the electoral system against these ongoing threats.

# Judicial Overreach: Stacking the Courts with Partisan Judges and Its Long-Term Implications for Democracy

The judiciary plays a crucial role in upholding the rule of law and ensuring that the principles of democracy are maintained. However, in recent years, there has been growing concern over the politicization of the judiciary, particularly through the strategic appointment of partisan judges. This process, often referred to as "court-packing" or judicial overreach, involves filling courts with judges who are perceived to be aligned with the political ideologies of those in power. This trend has significant implications for the independence of the judiciary and the long-term health of American democracy.

## *Strategic Appointments: Shaping the Judiciary to Serve Political Agendas*

The Importance of Judicial Appointments: Judicial appointments are one of the most enduring legacies a president can leave, as federal judges and Supreme Court justices serve lifetime appointments. This makes the selection of judges a highly strategic process, as these individuals can influence the interpretation of laws for decades, well beyond the tenure of the president who appointed them.

Republican Focus on the Judiciary: In recent decades, the Republican Party has placed a significant emphasis on shaping the judiciary. This focus became especially pronounced during the presidency of Donald Trump, who, with the support of Senate Majority Leader Mitch McConnell, successfully appointed over 230 federal judges, including three Supreme Court justices. These appointments were often made with the explicit goal of shifting the judiciary to the right, ensuring that conservative legal principles would dominate court rulings for generations.

Use of the Federalist Society: Many of Trump's judicial nominees were affiliated with the Federalist Society, a conservative legal organization that has played a key role in vetting and recommending candidates for judicial appointments. The organization's influence ensured that the judges appointed were not only conservative but also aligned with specific legal philosophies that emphasize limited government, originalism, and a narrow interpretation of individual rights, particularly in areas like reproductive rights and voting laws.

## *Supreme Court Shifts: From Moderation to a Conservative Supermajority*

The Impact of the Trump Era: The Trump administration's appointments to the Supreme Court Justices Neil Gorsuch, Brett Kavanaugh, and Amy Coney Barrett solidified a 6-3 conservative supermajority on the nation's highest court. This shift has had profound implications for key issues such as abortion rights, gun control, and the separation of church and state.

Overturning Precedents: The conservative majority on the Supreme Court has shown a willingness to overturn established precedents, as seen in the 2022 decision to overturn Roe v. Wade. This landmark ruling had protected abortion rights for nearly 50 years. This decision not only rolled back reproductive rights but also signaled that other longstanding precedents could be vulnerable, raising concerns about the stability and predictability of the law.

Future Implications: The conservative dominance of the Supreme Court is likely to influence American law and society for decades to come. With the potential to revisit and overturn decisions related to civil rights, voting rights, and environmental regulations, the court's trajectory threatens to reshape the legal landscape in ways that could undermine progressive policies and diminish the protection of individual rights.

## *Lower Courts: Expanding Conservative Influence Across the Judiciary*

Federal Appeals Courts: In addition to the Supreme Court, the stacking of federal appeals courts with conservative judges has had a significant impact on the judicial system. These courts, which handle the vast majority of federal cases, now reflect a conservative majority in many circuits, leading to rulings that align with Republican priorities on issues ranging from immigration to labor rights.

Judicial Activism: Conservative judges appointed to lower courts have been criticized for engaging in judicial activism, interpreting laws in ways that advance a specific political agenda rather than adhering to impartial legal principles. This has been evident in cases involving voting rights, where conservative judges have upheld restrictive voting laws and gerrymandered districts, contributing to the erosion of democratic norms.

Impact on Social Justice Issues: The conservative tilt in the judiciary has also affected social justice issues, with rulings that have weakened protections for LGBTQ+ rights, workers' rights, and environmental regulations. The long-term presence of these judges means that progressive legal challenges may face significant obstacles in the courts, slowing or reversing progress on social justice issues.

## Long-Term Implications for Democracy: Erosion of Judicial Independence

Undermining Checks and Balances: The stacking of the courts with partisan judges undermines the principle of judicial independence, which is essential for a healthy democracy. When the judiciary is perceived as an extension of a political party rather than an impartial arbiter of the law, public trust in the judicial system erodes. This perception weakens the judiciary's role as a check on executive and legislative power, leading to an imbalance in the separation of powers.

Polarization of the Judiciary: The increasing politicization of judicial appointments has contributed to the polarization of the judiciary, where judges are viewed more as political actors than as neutral enforcers of the law. This polarization can lead to more extreme and ideologically driven rulings, which may further divide the country and undermine the legitimacy of the courts.

Threats to Democratic Norms: The long-term implications of judicial overreach extend beyond individual rulings. As the judiciary becomes more partisan, the potential for rulings that undermine democratic norms, such as the protection of voting rights and the enforcement of checks on executive power, increases. This threatens the very foundation of American democracy, as the courts are increasingly used as tools to entrench the power of one party at the expense of democratic principles.

In Essence The stacking of the courts with partisan judges represents a significant challenge to the independence of the judiciary and the long-term health of American democracy. By filling the courts with judges who align with their political agenda, the Republican Party has not only shifted the legal landscape to the right but also raised concerns about the future of democratic governance in the United States. As the judiciary becomes more politicized, the potential for rulings that erode civil liberties, weaken checks and balances and undermine public trust in the courts grows, posing a serious threat to the principles upon which the nation was founded.

## Undermining the Free Press: Examining Efforts to Discredit and Control the Media, Restricting the Flow of Information

A free and independent press is often referred to as the "fourth estate," essential for holding power accountable and informing the public. However, recent years have seen an alarming trend toward undermining the free press, particularly by the Republican Party and its allies. This trend includes efforts to discredit the media, spread misinformation, and exert control over news outlets. These actions not only threaten the flow of accurate information but also pose a significant risk to the democratic process.

### *Discrediting the Media: Labeling the Press as "Enemy of the People"*

Erosion of Trust in Journalism: One of the most significant tactics used to undermine the free press has been the deliberate attempt to erode public trust in journalism. High-profile figures within the Republican Party, most notably former President Donald Trump, have frequently referred to the media as "fake news" and "the enemy of the people." These labels are designed to cast doubt on the credibility of the press, particularly outlets that report critically on the actions of the party or its leaders.

Impact on Public Perception: The constant vilification of the media has had a profound impact on public perception. Polls show that a significant portion of the American public, particularly those who identify with the Republican Party, have come to distrust mainstream news sources. This distrust creates an environment where misinformation and partisan narratives can flourish as people turn to alternative media outlets that reinforce their preexisting beliefs rather than seeking out objective information.

Chilling Effect on Journalism: The aggressive rhetoric against the press has also had a chilling effect on journalism. Reporters covering political events, especially those critical of the Republican Party, have faced harassment, threats, and, in some cases, physical violence. This hostile environment makes it more difficult for journalists to do their jobs, as they face increasing risks for holding power accountable.

## *Control and Manipulation of Media Outlets: Consolidating Power Over Information*

Media Ownership and Influence: Another tactic used to undermine the free press involves the consolidation of media ownership, where a few powerful individuals or corporations control a large portion of the news media. This concentration of media ownership has been leveraged by conservative interests to ensure that certain narratives dominate the news cycle. For example, conservative media moguls like Rupert Murdoch, who owns Fox News, have used their platforms to push partisan agendas, shaping public opinion in ways that align with Republican Party goals.

Promotion of Partisan Media: The rise of explicitly partisan media outlets, such as Fox News, Breitbart, and One America News Network (OANN), has further polarized the media landscape. These outlets often present news with a strong conservative bias, sometimes promoting conspiracy theories or misinformation to advance their political objectives. By offering an alternative to mainstream news, these outlets help to solidify the base of the Republican Party by reinforcing their worldview and dismissing opposing perspectives as illegitimate.

Suppressing Unfavorable Coverage: In addition to promoting favorable coverage, there have been efforts to suppress or discredit unfavorable coverage. This can involve pressuring media outlets to downplay or ignore stories that could damage the Republican Party's image. In some cases, this suppression takes the form of direct interference, such as when the Trump administration sought to revoke press credentials from journalists who asked tough questions or when Republican leaders criticized and attempted to defund public broadcasters like NPR and PBS, which are seen as more impartial.

## *Misinformation and Disinformation: Spreading False Narratives*

Deliberate Misinformation Campaigns: Misinformation and disinformation have become powerful tools for undermining the free press. By spreading false or misleading information, political actors can confuse the public, delegitimize the press, and divert attention from critical issues. Social media platforms have been particularly effective in amplifying these false narratives, allowing them to reach a wide audience quickly and with little oversight.

Weaponizing Social Media: The Republican Party and its allies have effectively used social media to spread misinformation and attack the credibility of traditional news sources. Whether through the dissemination of conspiracy theories, like those associated with QAnon, or through the strategic use of "alternative facts," social media has been weaponized to create echo chambers where falsehoods are accepted as truth. This undermines the role of the press as a source of reliable information and makes it harder for the public to distinguish between fact and fiction.

Consequences for Public Discourse: The spread of misinformation has serious consequences for public discourse. It creates divisions within society as people become more entrenched in their beliefs and less willing to engage with opposing viewpoints. This polarization weakens democratic debate and makes it more difficult for the press to fulfill its role as a facilitator of informed public discussion.

## *Legislative and Legal Threats: Undermining Press Freedom Through Policy*

Threats to Press Freedom: In addition to rhetorical attacks and misinformation, there have been legislative and legal efforts to undermine press freedom. These efforts include attempts to weaken libel laws, making it easier for public figures to sue journalists for unfavorable coverage. While framed as a way to protect individuals from defamation, such changes could have a chilling effect on investigative journalism, as news outlets may become more hesitant to publish critical stories for fear of costly legal battles.

Restricting Access to Information: Another way to undermine the free press is by restricting access to information. This can take the form of limiting journalists' access to government officials or withholding important documents and data that are necessary for accurate reporting. By controlling the flow of information, those in power can shape the narrative and prevent the public from learning about actions that may be detrimental to democracy.

Global Implications: The undermining of press freedom in the United States has global implications. As a country that has traditionally championed freedom of the press, the erosion of these principles at home sends a troubling signal to other nations. Authoritarian regimes around the world may feel encouraged to crack down on journalists and restrict press freedom in their own countries, citing the actions of the U.S. as justification.

In Essence The efforts to discredit, control, and undermine the free press represent a direct threat to the democratic process. By attacking the credibility of the media, consolidating control over information, spreading misinformation, and pursuing policies that restrict press freedom, the Republican Party and its allies are eroding one of the key pillars of democracy. The long-term implications of these actions are profound, as they weaken the ability of the press to hold power accountable, inform the public, and facilitate meaningful democratic debate. Without a free and independent press, the foundation of American democracy is at risk of crumbling, leading to a society where information is controlled, dissent is silenced, and the truth is increasingly difficult to discern.

# Chapter 3: Cult of Personality and the Strongman Leader

# Rise of the Strongman: How the Republican Party Has Embraced Leaders with Authoritarian Tendencies

In recent years, the Republican Party has increasingly gravitated towards leaders who exhibit strongman characteristics figures who project strength, assert control, and dismiss traditional democratic norms in favor of centralized, often authoritarian power. This shift reflects a significant departure from the party's historical values. It has profound implications for the future of American democracy. This section explores how and why the Republican Party has embraced these leaders, the tactics they use, and the potential consequences for the nation's political landscape.

## *Characteristics of the Strongman Leader: Centralizing Power and Undermining Democracy*

Authoritarian Traits: Strongman leaders typically exhibit a range of authoritarian traits, including a desire to centralize power, a disregard for institutional checks and balances, and a tendency to portray themselves as the sole protectors of the nation. These leaders often frame their actions as necessary to defend the country against internal and external threats, real or imagined and use this narrative to justify eroding democratic norms.

Populist Appeal: Strongman leaders frequently appeal to populist sentiments, positioning themselves as champions of the "common people" against corrupt elites. This populist rhetoric helps them build a loyal base of supporters who view them as protectors of national identity and traditional values. In the Republican Party, this has translated into a focus on issues like immigration, law and order, and national sovereignty, often at the expense of minority rights and democratic principles.

Disregard for Democratic Norms: These leaders often show a blatant disregard for democratic norms and institutions. They may undermine the judiciary, attack the free press, and challenge the legitimacy of elections when results do not favor them. By doing so, they weaken the foundational structures of democracy, making it easier to consolidate power and stifle dissent.

## *The Trump Phenomenon: A Case Study in Republican Strongman Leadership*

Donald Trump's Rise: The rise of Donald Trump as a central figure in the Republican Party marks the most significant example of the party's embrace of strongman leadership. Trump's 2016 presidential campaign was characterized by his promise to "Make America Great Again," a slogan that resonated with voters who felt left behind by globalization and social change. His brash style, willingness to disregard political norms, and attacks on the media and political opponents were key elements of his strongman appeal.

Trump's Authoritarian Tactics: During his presidency, Trump exhibited many hallmarks of authoritarian leadership. He frequently attacked the credibility of the press, dismissed the findings of intelligence agencies, and undermined the judiciary by questioning the impartiality of judges who ruled against him. Trump also sought to concentrate power in the executive branch, often bypassing Congress through executive orders and other unilateral actions. His refusal to accept the results of the 2020 presidential election, coupled with attempts to overturn the outcome, culminated in the January 6th Capitol insurrection, a stark demonstration of the dangers posed by strongman leadership.

Enduring Influence: Even after leaving office, Trump's influence within the Republican Party remains strong. His endorsement continues to be a powerful factor in Republican primaries, and many GOP leaders have aligned themselves with his brand of politics, echoing his rhetoric and adopting his combative style. This enduring influence underscores the party's ongoing shift towards embracing authoritarian tendencies.

## *Embracing Authoritarian Tactics: The GOP's Shift Towards Strongman Politics*

Loyalty to the Leader: A key feature of strongman politics is the demand for loyalty to the leader. Within the Republican Party, this has manifested in the expectation that party members demonstrate unwavering support for Trump and his agenda. Those who criticize or challenge him often face political retaliation, including primary challenges or public rebukes. This culture of loyalty has stifled dissent within the party and further entrenched the authoritarian tendencies of its leadership.

Weakening Democratic Institutions: The Republican Party's embrace of strongman leaders has led to efforts to weaken democratic institutions that serve as checks on executive power. This includes attempts to delegitimize elections, as seen in the widespread promotion of baseless claims of voter fraud following the 2020 election. By casting doubt on the integrity of the electoral process, the party has undermined public trust in democracy itself, paving the way for more authoritarian governance.

Legislative and Legal Maneuvers: In addition to rhetorical attacks on democracy, the Republican Party has supported legislative and legal maneuvers that concentrate power in the hands of the executive. For example, efforts to limit the independence of regulatory agencies, reduce the power of Congress to oversee the executive branch, and pack the judiciary with partisan judges all contribute to the erosion of democratic checks and balances. These moves align with the goals of strongman leaders, who seek to remove obstacles to their authority.

## Consequences for American Democracy: The Dangers of Strongman Rule

Erosion of Democratic Norms: The rise of strongman leadership within the Republican Party poses a serious threat to the norms and institutions that sustain American democracy. As these leaders consolidate power, they erode the rule of law, weaken the separation of powers, and undermine the principles of accountability and transparency. This erosion of norms makes it more difficult to hold leaders accountable and increases the risk of abuses of power.

Polarization and Division: Strongman leaders often thrive on polarization, using divisive rhetoric to mobilize their base and marginalize opponents. This deepens social and political divisions, making it harder to find common ground and weakening the sense of national unity. As the Republican Party continues to embrace strongman politics, the polarization of American society is likely to intensify, leading to increased conflict and instability.

Threat to Civil Liberties: The authoritarian tendencies of strongman leaders also pose a direct threat to civil liberties. In their quest for control, these leaders may seek to curtail freedom of speech, freedom of the press, and the right to protest. The Republican Party's increasing tolerance for such tactics raises concerns about the future of civil rights and individual freedoms in the United States.

In Essence The Republican Party's embrace of strongman leadership represents a significant departure from its historical values and poses a serious challenge to American democracy. By rallying around leaders who centralize power, disregard democratic norms, and demand loyalty, the party has moved toward an authoritarian model of governance. This shift has profound implications for the future of the United States, threatening the foundational principles of democracy and the stability of the nation. As the influence of strongman leaders grows within the party, the risks to civil liberties, political unity, and democratic governance become increasingly severe, raising urgent questions about the direction of American politics.

## Cult of Personality: How Loyalty to a Single Leader Has Overshadowed Party Principles and Democratic Norms

A defining characteristic of strongman politics is the emergence of a cult of personality, where loyalty to a single leader eclipses traditional party principles and even democratic norms. Within the Republican Party, this phenomenon has become increasingly evident, as unwavering allegiance to figures like Donald Trump has taken precedence over the party's historical values and the foundational principles of American democracy. This section explores the rise of the cult of personality in the GOP, its implications for the party and the nation, and the dangers it poses to democratic governance.

### *The Rise of the Cult of Personality: Centralizing Power Around a Single Leader*

Personal Loyalty Over Principles: The cult of personality in the Republican Party has manifested in the prioritization of personal loyalty to the leader over adherence to the party's traditional principles. Rather than focusing on conservative values like limited government, individual freedoms, and fiscal responsibility, the party has increasingly rallied around the persona of its leader. This shift reflects a deeper transformation in the GOP, where the leader's brand and rhetoric have become the primary unifying force.

Leader as the Party's Identity: In a cult of personality, the leader's identity becomes synonymous with the party itself. This has been particularly evident in the case of Donald Trump, whose influence over the Republican Party has been so profound that the party's platform in the 2020 election was essentially reduced to supporting his agenda. The GOP's embrace of Trump's "Make America Great Again" slogan and its willingness to follow his lead, even when it contradicts longstanding conservative positions, highlights how the party's identity has become intertwined with that of its leader.

## *Mechanisms of Control: Enforcing Loyalty Through Pressure and Retaliation*

Political Retaliation Against Dissenters: One of the key mechanisms through which the cult of personality is maintained is the enforcement of loyalty through pressure and retaliation. Republican leaders and lawmakers who criticize or oppose the leader often face swift and severe consequences. This can include being ostracized by the party, facing primary challenges backed by the leader's supporters, or being publicly denounced by the leader himself. The case of Liz Cheney, who was removed from her leadership position in the House GOP after condemning Trump's actions related to the January 6th insurrection, is a clear example of how dissent is punished within the party.

Pressure to Conform: The cult of personality also exerts pressure on party members to conform to the leader's views and directives, even when they conflict with their own beliefs or the party's traditional values. This pressure is reinforced by the leader's ability to mobilize a loyal base of supporters who demand loyalty to their chosen figure. For many Republican lawmakers, the fear of losing support from this base has led to a reluctance to challenge the leader, even in cases where doing so would align with their principles or protect democratic norms.

## *Erosion of Democratic Norms: The Dangers of Loyalty Over Principle*

Undermining Democratic Institutions: The prioritization of loyalty to a single leader over democratic principles has serious implications for the health of American democracy. When party members are more concerned with maintaining favor with the leader than with upholding democratic norms, institutions designed to check and balance power can be weakened or ignored. This was evident in the GOP's response to Trump's refusal to accept the results of the 2020 election, where many Republicans supported or remained silent on his baseless claims of voter fraud, undermining the integrity of the electoral process.

Weakening the Rule of Law: The cult of personality also poses a threat to the rule of law, as leaders who loyal followers insulate may feel emboldened to act with impunity. This can lead to actions that disregard legal constraints, such as attempts to interfere with ongoing investigations, pressure on judicial processes, or efforts to bypass legislative authority. The Republican Party's support for Trump's controversial actions, such as his efforts to pressure Ukraine to investigate a political rival or his attempts to influence the Department of Justice, illustrate how the rule of law can be compromised when loyalty to the leader is placed above accountability.

## *Impact on the Republican Party: Transformation and Division*

Shifting Party Identity: The rise of the cult of personality has fundamentally transformed the identity of the Republican Party. While the party was once a broad coalition of conservative, libertarian, and centrist factions united by shared principles, it has increasingly become a vehicle for the personal ambitions of its leader. This shift has led to internal divisions, as traditional conservatives and those who value democratic norms find themselves at odds with the party's new direction. The departure of high-profile Republicans who opposed Trump, such as former Senators Jeff Flake and Bob Corker, highlights the extent of this transformation.

Long-Term Consequences: The long-term consequences of the cult of personality within the GOP are uncertain but potentially far-reaching. The party's reliance on a single leader for its identity and direction may leave it vulnerable to fragmentation if that leader falls from favor or is no longer able to maintain control. Additionally, the erosion of traditional conservative principles and democratic norms may alienate segments of the electorate who are uncomfortable with the party's authoritarian tendencies, leading to potential electoral losses and further polarization.

### *The Broader Impact on American Democracy: A Dangerous Precedent*

Setting a Precedent for Future Leaders: The embrace of a cult of personality sets a dangerous precedent for future leaders, both within the Republican Party and beyond. By demonstrating that loyalty to a leader can outweigh adherence to democratic principles, the party risks normalizing authoritarian behavior and encouraging other political figures to adopt similar tactics. This could lead to a broader erosion of democratic norms across the political spectrum, with serious implications for the stability and integrity of American democracy.

Challenges to Rebuilding Democratic Norms: Reversing the damage caused by the cult of personality will be a significant challenge for the Republican Party and for American democracy as a whole. Restoring a commitment to democratic principles, such as the rule of law, checks and balances, and respect for institutions, will require a concerted effort by party leaders, lawmakers, and the electorate. It will also require a willingness to confront and reject the authoritarian tendencies that have taken root within the party, even at the risk of short-term political costs.

In Essence The rise of a cult of personality within the Republican Party represents a profound shift in the party's identity and a significant threat to American democracy. As loyalty to a single leader has come to overshadow traditional party principles and democratic norms, the GOP has increasingly aligned itself with authoritarian tendencies that undermine the rule of law, weaken democratic institutions, and threaten the stability of the nation. The long-term consequences of this shift are likely to be felt not only within the Republican Party but across the entire political landscape, as the normalization of authoritarian behavior sets a dangerous precedent for future leaders and challenges the very foundations of American democracy.

## Impact on Governance: How the Focus on a Strongman Leader Affects Policy-Making and the Balance of Power

The rise of a strongman leader within the Republican Party has not only transformed the party's identity but also significantly impacted governance in the United States. The focus on a single, powerful leader reshapes how policies are made, implemented, and enforced, often undermining the traditional balance of power that is central to American democracy. This section examines how the centralization of power in a strongman leader affects policy-making, the role of institutions, and the overall balance of power within the government.

### *Centralization of Power: Eroding Checks and Balances*

Executive Dominance: In a system where a strongman leader is the focal point, power increasingly shifts towards the executive branch. This centralization of authority diminishes the role of Congress and the judiciary, which are traditionally designed to act as checks on executive power. Strongman leaders often bypass legislative processes, relying heavily on executive orders, decrees, and other unilateral actions to push their agenda. This undermines the principle of separation of powers, leading to an imbalance in governance where the executive branch dominates policy-making.

Marginalization of Legislative Input: As the executive branch consolidates power, the legislative branch often finds its role in policy-making diminished. Strongman leaders may disregard or undermine Congress's authority by sidestepping the legislative process, pressuring lawmakers to align with their agenda, or using tactics like government shutdowns to force compliance. This marginalization weakens the ability of Congress to serve as a co-equal branch of government. It reduces its capacity to represent the diverse interests of the American public.

## Policy-Making Driven by Loyalty: Prioritizing the Leader's Agenda Over Public Interest

Loyalty Over Expertise: In a governance system dominated by a strongman leader, loyalty to the leader often becomes more important than expertise or the public interest in policy-making. Key positions within the government may be filled with individuals who are chosen not for their qualifications or experience but for their unwavering loyalty to the leader. This can result in policies that are more about advancing the leader's personal or political goals than addressing the needs of the country. The quality of governance suffers as a result, with decisions being made based on political expediency rather than sound policy analysis.

Short-Term Focus: Strongman leaders tend to prioritize policies that deliver immediate, visible results, often to reinforce their image as decisive and effective. This short-term focus can lead to the implementation of policies that are popular with the leader's base but may have detrimental long-term consequences. For example, tax cuts that benefit the wealthy or deregulation that favors certain industries may boost the leader's popularity in the short run but contribute to economic inequality or environmental degradation in the long term.

## Erosion of Institutional Independence: Undermining the Role of Key Agencies

Politicization of Institutions: Under strongman leadership, the independence of key government institutions is often compromised. Agencies that are supposed to operate based on objective criteria and expertise may be pressured to align with the leader's political agenda. For instance, regulatory agencies might be directed to relax rules that inconvenience the leader's allies, or law enforcement agencies may be used to target political opponents. This politicization erodes public trust in these institutions and diminishes their ability to function effectively.

Judicial Manipulation: The judiciary, which traditionally acts as a check on executive overreach, can also come under threat in a strongman-dominated system. Strongman leaders often seek to stack the courts with judges who are sympathetic to their views, undermining the judiciary's independence. This can lead to a situation where the courts are less likely to challenge unconstitutional actions by the executive branch, further consolidating the leader's power and eroding the rule of law.

## *Impact on Governance: Challenges to Effective and Accountable Government*

Undermining Accountability: In a system centered around a strongman leader, accountability mechanisms are often weakened or circumvented. The leader may dismiss or discredit oversight bodies, such as inspectors general or ethics committees, that are tasked with holding the executive branch accountable. This lack of accountability can lead to corruption, abuse of power, and decisions that are not in the public interest. The absence of effective checks on the leader's power creates an environment where governance becomes less transparent and more prone to authoritarianism.

Policy Inconsistency: The focus on a single leader's agenda can also lead to inconsistency in policy-making. As the leader's priorities shift or as different factions within the leader's inner circle gain influence, policies may be reversed, altered, or implemented haphazardly. This inconsistency can create confusion, disrupt long-term planning, and undermine the stability of government programs. It also makes it difficult for other branches of government, as well as the private sector and civil society, to anticipate and respond to policy changes.

## *Consequences for Democracy: The Risk of Authoritarian Governance*

Weakening Democratic Norms: The centralization of power in a strongman leader weakens the democratic norms that underpin American governance. As the leader's influence grows, the principles of compromise, deliberation, and consensus-building that are essential to democracy become sidelined. Governance becomes more autocratic, with decisions being made by a small group of loyalists rather than through inclusive and transparent processes. This shift erodes public confidence in democratic institutions and can lead to increased political polarization and instability.

Threats to Civil Liberties: Strongman leaders often prioritize security and order over civil liberties, leading to policies that restrict freedom of speech, assembly, and the press. The use of state power to suppress dissent, silence critics, and control the flow of information poses a serious threat to individual rights and freedoms. In the long run, these authoritarian tendencies can undermine the very foundation of democracy, making it harder to reverse the concentration of power and restore a healthy, functioning democratic system.

In Essence The focus on a strongman leader within the Republican Party has far-reaching implications for governance in the United States. By centralizing power in the executive branch, prioritizing loyalty over principles, and undermining institutional independence, this approach to governance challenges the traditional balance of power that is essential to American democracy. The result is a system where policy-making is driven by the leader's agenda rather than the public interest, accountability is weakened, and democratic norms are eroded. As the influence of strongman leadership grows, the risks to effective, transparent, and accountable governance become increasingly severe, posing a significant threat to the future of American democracy.

# Chapter 4: Suppression of Dissent and Opposition

## Silencing Critics: How Dissent Within the Party and the Broader Political Sphere Is Being Stifled

A hallmark of authoritarian leadership is the suppression of dissent, both within the ruling party and across the broader political landscape. Within the Republican Party and American politics more generally, there has been a growing trend of silencing critics who challenge the dominant narrative or oppose the strongman leader. This section explores the tactics used to stifle dissent, the consequences for democratic discourse, and the broader implications for the health of American democracy.

### *Internal Party Suppression: Enforcing Loyalty Through Fear and Retaliation*

Ostracizing Dissenters: Within the Republican Party, there has been a marked effort to ostracize and marginalize members who challenge the party's leadership or its direction. Lawmakers and party officials who criticize the leader or deviate from the party line often face swift retaliation. This can include losing committee assignments, being stripped of leadership roles, or facing primary challenges backed by the party leadership or the leader's supporters. The case of Representative Liz Cheney, who was removed from her position as House Republican Conference Chair after criticizing Donald Trump's actions related to the January 6th insurrection, is a clear example of how dissent is punished within the party.

Fear of Repercussions: The fear of facing similar consequences has led to a culture of silence within the party, where many members choose to remain silent rather than risk their political careers by speaking out. This atmosphere stifles open debate and discussion, which are essential for a healthy democratic process. Instead of engaging in meaningful dialogue about the direction of the party and the nation, lawmakers are pressured to conform to the leader's views, even when they conflict with their principles or the interests of their constituents.

## *Control Over the Broader Political Discourse: Undermining Opponents and Critics*

Discrediting the Opposition: In the broader political sphere, strongman leaders often seek to discredit their opponents and critics rather than engage with their arguments. This can involve labeling them as â€œenemies of the people,â€ questioning their patriotism, or accusing them of being part of a conspiracy to undermine the leader. These tactics are designed to delegitimize dissent and create an environment where opposing views are dismissed without consideration. By attacking the credibility of critics rather than addressing their concerns, strongman leaders can stifle meaningful debate and discourage others from speaking out.

Weaponizing Social Media: Social media has become a powerful tool for silencing critics, as strongman leaders and their supporters use these platforms to launch coordinated attacks on those who oppose them. Critics may be subjected to harassment, threats, and character assassination campaigns designed to intimidate them into silence. The spread of misinformation and disinformation on social media further exacerbates this problem, as false narratives are used to discredit critics and create confusion among the public. This weaponization of social media not only stifles dissent but also undermines the integrity of public discourse.

## *Restricting Media Freedom: Controlling the Narrative*

Attacks on the Free Press: A free and independent press is a cornerstone of democracy, but it often comes under attack in systems dominated by strongman leaders. Leaders who seek to silence dissent frequently target the media, accusing journalists of bias, spreading â€œfake news,â€ or working against the national interest. These attacks are designed to undermine the public's trust in the media and create a climate where only the leader's narrative is seen as legitimate. By discrediting the press, strongman leaders can control the flow of information, making it harder for the public to access unbiased news and critical perspectives.

Legal and Financial Pressure: In addition to rhetorical attacks, strongman leaders may use legal and financial pressure to suppress media outlets that are critical of their administration. This can include lawsuits, regulatory actions, or the withdrawal of government advertising to weaken independent media financially. In some cases, media owners may be pressured to sell their outlets to individuals or entities aligned with the leader, further consolidating control over the narrative. These tactics create an environment where journalists may censor themselves or avoid reporting on sensitive issues to avoid retaliation, leading to a less informed public.

## *Impact on Civil Society: Marginalizing Activists and Advocacy Groups*

Targeting Activists: Activists and advocacy groups that challenge the strongman leader's policies or advocate for marginalized communities are often targeted for suppression. This can include surveillance, harassment, or legal action aimed at intimidating activists and discouraging them from organizing. In some cases, leaders may label activist groups as â€œextremistsâ€ or â€œterroristsâ€ to justify crackdowns on their activities. These efforts to marginalize civil society weaken the capacity of citizens to organize, advocate for their rights, and hold the government accountable.

Erosion of Public Space: The suppression of dissent also extends to the public space, where peaceful protests and demonstrations may be met with excessive force or legal restrictions. Strongman leaders may use public order laws, curfews, or emergency powers to limit the ability of citizens to gather and express their views. The use of law enforcement or even military forces to break up protests can create a climate of fear where people are reluctant to participate in public demonstrations. This erosion of public space for dissent further undermines democratic participation. It stifles the voices of those who oppose the government's actions.

## *Consequences for Democracy: The Dangers of Silencing Dissent*

Undermining Democratic Principles: The suppression of dissent is antithetical to the principles of democracy, which rely on open debate, free expression, and the ability of citizens to hold their leaders accountable. When dissent is stifled, the quality of democratic governance suffers, as alternative perspectives are ignored and policies go unchallenged. This can lead to the entrenchment of bad policies, corruption, and abuses of power, as there are fewer checks on the actions of those in power.

Polarization and Division: Silencing critics also contributes to increased political polarization and division. When dissenting voices are marginalized or discredited, the political discourse becomes more extreme, with little room for compromise or consensus-building. This polarization can lead to social unrest, as marginalized groups and individuals who feel unheard may resort to more radical forms of protest or disengage from the political process altogether. The result is a more fragmented society, where trust in democratic institutions erodes and the potential for conflict increases.

In Essence The silencing of critics within the Republican Party and the broader political sphere represents a significant threat to American democracy. By stifling dissent, strongman leaders undermine the principles of open debate, free expression, and accountability that are essential for healthy democratic governance. The consequences of this suppression are far-reaching, affecting not only the quality of policy-making but also the overall stability and cohesion of society. As dissenting voices are silenced, the risks of authoritarianism, corruption, and social division grow, posing a serious challenge to the future of democracy in the United States.

## Criminalization of Protest: Laws and Policies Aimed at Suppressing Protests and Political Opposition

Protest is a fundamental democratic right, serving as a crucial mechanism for citizens to express their grievances, demand accountability, and advocate for change. However, in recent years, there has been a growing trend toward the criminalization of protest, where laws and policies are specifically designed to suppress public demonstrations and stifle political opposition. This section examines the ways in which protests are being criminalized, the motivations behind these actions, and the broader implications for civil liberties and democracy.

## *New Legislation Targeting Protesters*

Increased Penalties: Across various states, there has been a surge in the introduction of laws that impose harsher penalties on protesters. These laws often redefine what constitutes illegal activity during protests, broadening the scope to include actions like blocking traffic, trespassing on public property, or even organizing a protest without proper permits. The penalties for these offenses have been significantly increased, with some states introducing felony charges for actions that were previously considered misdemeanors. This escalation in penalties serves as a deterrent, discouraging people from participating in protests out of fear of severe legal consequences.

Anti-Riot Laws: Some states have passed or proposed â€œanti-riotâ€ laws that are broadly defined, making it easier to charge peaceful protesters with rioting if any violence or property damage occurs during a demonstration, even if the majority of participants were peaceful. These laws often allow for collective punishment, where individuals can be held accountable for the actions of others, leading to a chilling effect on public participation in protests. By blurring the lines between peaceful protest and violent unrest, these laws create a legal environment that criminalizes dissent and suppresses legitimate political expression.

## *Expanding Law Enforcement Powers*

Militarization of the Police: In response to protests, there has been a noticeable increase in the militarization of law enforcement. Police forces are increasingly equipped with military-grade weapons, armored vehicles, and other tools typically used in combat situations. This militarization is justified as a means of maintaining public order. Still, it often results in the excessive use of force against protesters. The presence of heavily armed police at protests can escalate tensions and lead to violent confrontations, further criminalizing the act of protest itself.

Surveillance and Monitoring: Law enforcement agencies have also expanded their use of surveillance technologies to monitor protests and track the activities of activists. This includes the use of drones, facial recognition software, and social media monitoring to identify and target individuals involved in organizing or participating in protests. The widespread use of surveillance not only invades the privacy of protesters but also creates a sense of fear and intimidation, discouraging people from engaging in political activism. The data collected through these methods can be used to justify arrests, charge individuals with crimes, or build cases against protest organizers, further criminalizing the right to protest.

## Chilling Effect on Free Speech and Assembly

Deterring Participation: The criminalization of protest has a profound chilling effect on the exercise of free speech and the right to assemble. When people are faced with the possibility of arrest, harsh penalties, or police violence, they may be less likely to participate in protests or engage in other forms of political activism. This self-censorship weakens civil society's ability to advocate for change and hold the government accountable. The fear of reprisal can lead to a decline in public demonstrations, making it easier for those in power to avoid scrutiny and resist demands for reform.

Targeting Marginalized Communities: The criminalization of protest disproportionately affects marginalized communities, which are often at the forefront of movements for social and political change. Black Lives Matter protests, Indigenous land rights demonstrations, and environmental activism are just a few examples of movements that have faced heightened repression. By targeting these communities, the criminalization of protest reinforces existing inequalities. It silences the voices of those who are most impacted by systemic injustice. The result is a narrowing of the democratic space, where only the views of the privileged or the compliant are heard.

## Legal and Political Justifications

Framing Protests as Threats: One of the key strategies used to justify the criminalization of protest is framing demonstrations as threats to public safety or national security. This rhetoric is often employed by government officials to paint protesters as dangerous radicals or violent agitators, even when the vast majority of participants are peaceful. By framing protests in this way, authorities can justify the use of heavy-handed tactics and restrictive laws under the guise of protecting the public. This narrative not only delegitimizes the protesters' grievances but also shifts the focus away from the issues they are advocating for, further marginalizing dissenting voices.

Political Motives: The criminalization of protest is often driven by political motives, particularly when protests challenge the policies or actions of those in power. Leaders who feel threatened by mass mobilization may seek to suppress protests to maintain their authority and avoid accountability. This is particularly evident in situations where protests are directed against government corruption, police brutality, or environmental destruction. By criminalizing protest, political leaders can stifle opposition, prevent the spread of dissent, and maintain the status quo, even when it goes against the will of the people.

## *Broader Implications for Democracy*

Erosion of Civil Liberties: The criminalization of protest represents a significant erosion of civil liberties, particularly the rights to free speech, assembly, and association. When the state uses its power to suppress dissent, it undermines the foundational principles of democracy, where citizens are supposed to have the freedom to express their views and demand change. The loss of these rights weakens the ability of civil society to function effectively. It diminishes the capacity of individuals to influence the political process.

Weakening of Democratic Institutions: The criminalization of protest also has long-term implications for the health of democratic institutions. As the state becomes more authoritarian in its response to dissent, the balance of power shifts increasingly in favor of the executive branch, with less oversight from the judiciary or the legislature. This concentration of power undermines the checks and balances that are essential for democratic governance and opens the door to further abuses of power. Over time, the suppression of protest can lead to a more repressive political environment, where opposition is systematically crushed and democratic norms are eroded.

In Essence The criminalization of protest is a troubling trend that poses a serious threat to democracy in the United States. Through the use of harsh laws, expanded police powers, and political rhetoric, the right to protest is being systematically suppressed. This not only stifles dissent but also undermines the fundamental principles of free speech and assembly that are central to a healthy democracy. As protests are increasingly criminalized, the voices of marginalized communities are silenced, civil liberties are eroded, and the balance of power is skewed in favor of those who seek to maintain the status quo. The long-term consequences of this trend are profound, as it weakens the ability of citizens to hold their government accountable and risks pushing the country further toward authoritarianism.

## Weaponizing the Law: How Legal Systems Are Used to Target Political Opponents and Critics

The use of legal systems to target political opponents and critics often referred to as "weaponizing the law," is a powerful tool in the arsenal of authoritarian leaders. This tactic involves the strategic application of laws, legal procedures, and judicial processes to intimidate, discredit, or outright eliminate political challengers and dissenting voices. By manipulating the law, those in power can maintain their dominance while giving the appearance of legality and due process. This section delves into the methods, motivations, and consequences of weaponizing the law, particularly in the context of recent political developments.

### *Selective Prosecution: Targeting Political Opponents*

Criminal Charges as Political Weapons: One of the most direct ways the law is weaponized is through the selective prosecution of political opponents. Legal authorities may bring charges against opposition leaders, activists, or critics based on exaggerated or fabricated allegations. These charges can range from corruption and fraud to more nebulous accusations like â€œinciting violenceâ€ or â€œthreatening national security.â€ The goal is not necessarily to secure a conviction but to tarnish the reputation of the target, drain their resources, and keep them entangled in lengthy legal battles.

Examples of Selective Prosecution: There have been numerous instances where political figures who challenge the status quo find themselves facing sudden legal scrutiny. In some cases, these prosecutions are based on minor infractions that are blown out of proportion. In contrast, in others, the charges are entirely spurious. The legal process itself becomes the punishment, as individuals are forced to spend time and money defending themselves, often in a highly publicized and damaging manner. The use of the law in this way creates an uneven playing field, where political competition is not based on ideas or policies but on who can survive legal harassment.

## Legal Harassment: Burdening Critics with Lawsuits and Investigations

Strategic Lawsuits Against Public Participation (SLAPPs): Legal harassment often takes the form of SLAPPs lawsuits filed with the intention of silencing or intimidating critics. These suits are typically baseless or exaggerated but are used to burden the defendant with the cost and stress of a legal defense. Activists, journalists, and whistleblowers are common targets of SLAPPs, which can be used to discourage them from speaking out or engaging in public advocacy. Even if the lawsuit is eventually dismissed, the financial and emotional toll on the defendant can be significant, leading to a chilling effect on free speech and activism.

Endless Investigations: In addition to lawsuits, political opponents and critics may be subjected to continuous investigations, often with no clear endpoint. These investigations can be launched by government agencies, legislative bodies, or independent commissions and are often used to create a cloud of suspicion around the target. The mere existence of an investigation can be damaging, as it suggests wrongdoing, even if no evidence is ultimately found. By keeping critics under constant scrutiny, those in power can undermine their credibility and distract them from their work while also sending a message to others about the risks of opposition.

## Manipulating the Judiciary: Ensuring Favorable Legal Outcomes

Stacking the Courts: To weaponize the law effectively, it is often necessary to ensure that the judiciary is sympathetic to the goals of those in power. This can be achieved through the strategic appointment of judges who are aligned with the ruling party or leader's ideology. Once in place, these judges can be relied upon to issue rulings that favor the government's interests, whether that means upholding controversial laws, dismissing cases against political allies, or convicting opponents on flimsy evidence. The stacking of the courts undermines the independence of the judiciary. It erodes public trust in the legal system as a neutral arbiter of justice.

Politicized Prosecutions and Pardons: The manipulation of the judiciary is often accompanied by politicized prosecutions and the selective use of pardons. Politicized prosecutions involve bringing charges against opponents for the express purpose of eliminating them from the political arena. At the same time, pardons can be used to protect allies who have committed crimes in service of the ruling party or leader. These actions create a dual system of justice, where the law is applied unevenly, depending on political affiliation. This not only undermines the rule of law but also erodes the legitimacy of legal institutions, as they are seen as tools of political power rather than protectors of justice.

## *Using National Security Laws to Suppress Dissent*

Broad and Vague Legislation: National security laws are often written in broad and vague terms, allowing them to be used against a wide range of activities that the government deems threatening. These laws can criminalize actions that would otherwise be protected by free speech or assembly rights, such as protesting, organizing, or publishing critical material. Under the guise of protecting national security, governments can use these laws to crack down on opposition and silence critics, particularly during times of political unrest or crisis. The vague nature of these laws makes them highly versatile tools for suppressing dissent, as they can be interpreted in ways that suit the government's needs.

Labeling Opponents as National Security Threats: Another common tactic is to label political opponents, activists, or journalists as threats to national security. By framing dissent as a danger to the state, the government can justify extreme measures, such as surveillance, detention without trial, or even torture. This tactic is particularly effective in creating public support for repressive actions, as citizens may be more willing to accept restrictions on civil liberties if they believe it is necessary for their safety. The use of national security as a pretext for targeting opponents allows governments to bypass normal legal protections and operate with greater impunity.

## *Consequences for Democracy and Civil Liberties*

Erosion of Trust in Legal Institutions: The weaponization of the law erodes public trust in legal institutions, as they are increasingly seen as instruments of political power rather than impartial guardians of justice. When the law is used to target opponents and protect allies, it undermines the principle of equal justice under the law. It contributes to a sense of cynicism and disillusionment among the public. This erosion of trust can have long-term consequences for the stability of democratic institutions as citizens lose faith in the fairness and integrity of the legal system.

Chilling Effect on Political Participation: The fear of legal retribution can have a chilling effect on political participation, as individuals and groups may be deterred from engaging in activism, running for office, or speaking out against the government. When the law is weaponized, the risks of political engagement become higher, and only the most privileged or courageous are willing to challenge the status quo. This narrowing of the political space weakens democracy, as it reduces the diversity of voices and perspectives in the public sphere and allows those in power to operate with less accountability.

In Essence The weaponization of the law represents a significant threat to democracy and the rule of law. By using legal systems to target political opponents and critics, those in power can maintain their dominance while undermining the principles of fairness, justice, and equality before the law. The consequences of this trend are far-reaching, as they weaken the integrity of legal institutions, erode public trust, and stifle political participation as the law becomes a tool of repression rather than a protector of rights, the foundations of democracy are undermined, paving the way for authoritarianism and the erosion of civil liberties.

# Chapter 5: Manipulation of Public Opinion

# Misinformation and Propaganda: The Impact on Public Opinion and Democratic Discourse

In contemporary politics, misinformation, conspiracy theories, and propaganda have become pervasive tools used to manipulate public opinion and distort democratic discourse. These elements not only mislead the public but also deepen societal divisions, erode trust in institutions, and undermine the principles of democratic deliberation. This section explores the roles and consequences of misinformation and propaganda, particularly how they are used to influence political outcomes and the broader implications for democracy.

## *The Spread of Misinformation: Sources and Mechanisms*

Digital Platforms as Amplifiers: The rise of digital platforms has dramatically increased the speed and scope with which misinformation can spread. Social media, blogs, and online forums serve as echo chambers where false information is amplified without adequate checks. The algorithms that underpin these platforms prioritize content that is sensational or emotionally charged, regardless of its truthfulness, leading to a rapid dissemination of misinformation.

Role of Partisan Media: Partisan media outlets also play a crucial role in spreading misinformation. These outlets create narratives that reflect the biases of their target audiences, often disregarding facts in favor of sensationalism. By presenting skewed versions of events or outright falsehoods, partisan media contribute to a polarized media landscape where audiences are insulated from balanced perspectives and are instead fed a steady diet of confirmation bias.

## *Conspiracy Theories: Creation, Circulation, and Impact*

Origins and Appeal: Conspiracy theories often arise during periods of uncertainty or societal stress, offering simple explanations for complex events. These theories typically identify scapegoats (e.g., political opponents, government institutions, minority groups) and allege secret plots, appealing to the fears and prejudices of certain segments of the population. The inherent drama of conspiracy narratives makes them particularly attractive and resilient to disproof.

Tools for Political Manipulation: Politicians and interest groups sometimes exploit conspiracy theories to discredit opponents and rally support. By endorsing or tacitly supporting these theories, political figures can galvanize their base, divert attention from substantive issues, and delegitimize the opposition. This tactic can be particularly effective in undermining public trust in electoral processes, public health initiatives, or any area where policies are contested.

## Propaganda Techniques: Shaping Perceptions and Attitudes

Emotional Manipulation: Propaganda leverages emotional manipulation to shape attitudes and behaviors. It often employs fear, anger, pride, or hope to reinforce loyalty to a cause or hostility towards an opposition. By appealing to emotions rather than reason, propaganda bypasses critical thinking, making individuals more susceptible to accepting misleading or false information.

Repetition and Saturation: Repetition is a key technique in propaganda, as repeated exposure to a message tends to increase its acceptance as truth. By saturating media with specific talking points or images, propagandists can create an aura of ubiquity and inevitability around certain ideas, making dissent seem isolated or irrelevant.

Simplification and Scapegoating: Propaganda simplifies complex issues into binary choices, good versus evil narratives, and clear us-versus-them distinctions. This simplification reduces the space for nuanced debate and critical discussion, pushing the public towards extremism. Scapegoating, a related technique, assigns blame to specific groups for broader societal problems, deflecting responsibility and fostering division.

## Implications for Democracy: Erosion of Informed Citizenry

Undermining Rational Discourse: The prevalence of misinformation and propaganda undermines the possibility of rational discourse, a cornerstone of democratic decision-making. When falsehoods and emotionally charged content dominate public debate, it becomes difficult for citizens to make informed decisions or engage in meaningful discussions about policy choices.

Eroding Trust in Institutions: Misinformation and conspiracy theories often target public institutions, accusing them of incompetence or malice. This sustained attack erodes trust in institutions essential for democracy, such as the media, courts, electoral bodies, and scientific organizations. As trust declines, so does public engagement and support for democratic governance.

Polarization and Fragmentation: The divisive nature of misinformation and propaganda contributes to political polarization, making compromise and consensus increasingly difficult. Societies become fragmented, with each segment clinging to its version of reality. This fragmentation poses significant challenges to collective action and societal cohesion, essential elements for a stable democracy.

## Countermeasures and the Path Forward

Media Literacy and Public Education: Enhancing media literacy among the populace is crucial in combating misinformation. Educational programs that teach individuals to evaluate sources critically, recognize biased reporting, and check facts can empower citizens to navigate the information landscape more effectively.

Regulatory and Technological Solutions: Governments and platforms must collaborate to find regulatory and technological solutions that balance freedom of expression with the need to curb misinformation. This might include better content moderation practices, transparency in algorithmic decision-making, and the promotion of fact-checking services.

Civic Engagement and Open Dialogue: Encouraging civic engagement and open dialogue can help bridge divides and counteract the effects of misinformation. Initiatives that bring together diverse groups to discuss common issues in structured settings can promote understanding and reduce susceptibility to divisive propaganda.

In Essence Misinformation, conspiracy theories, and propaganda represent significant threats to the health of democratic societies. They distort public opinion, undermine trust in institutions, and polarize communities, making it challenging to govern effectively or uphold democratic norms. Addressing these challenges requires a concerted effort that combines education, regulation, and active engagement from all sectors of society. By promoting a culture of critical thinking and open dialogue, democracies can hope to counteract these pernicious influences and foster a more informed and cohesive public sphere.

## Dividing the Nation: How Fear, Division, and Identity Politics Are Used to Consolidate Power

The use of fear, division, and identity politics as strategies to consolidate political power has become increasingly prevalent in modern political landscapes. By amplifying societal divisions and exploiting cultural, racial, or economic anxieties, political leaders and parties can strengthen their hold on power while undermining the principles of inclusive democracy. This section explores how these tactics are employed, the psychological and social mechanisms behind them, and the profound implications they have for democratic governance.

### *Exploiting Fear and Insecurity*

Fear as a Political Tool: Fear is a powerful motivator in human behavior, and politicians frequently exploit it to gain or maintain power. Leaders may emphasize perceived threats, whether economic, social, or security-related, to create a sense of urgency or crisis that justifies extraordinary measures or the need for strong leadership. This can include the exaggeration of national security threats, the demonization of immigrants as dangers to societal well-being, or the portrayal of economic policies as existential threats to specific groups of citizens.

Emergency Powers and Control: In response to these cultivated fears, leaders often seek expanded powers to deal with the supposed crises. These powers might include increased surveillance, restrictions on protests, or other measures that curtail civil liberties. The argument is typically framed in a way that these steps are necessary to protect the nation. Still, in practice, they can be used to suppress dissent and strengthen authoritarian control.

## Sowing Division: Us vs. Them Dynamics

Polarization Through Identity Politics: Identity politics can be a double-edged sword. While it can empower marginalized groups, it can also be manipulated to sow division. Politicians might emphasize differences rather than commonalities, creating stark 'us versus them' narratives. This can be based on race, religion, ethnicity, nationality, or social status. By highlighting these divisions, leaders can rally their base by positioning themselves as protectors of one group's interests against another, which they claim are mutually incompatible.

Consolidation of In-Group Loyalty: The division strategy helps consolidate in-group loyalty by fostering a strong sense of identity and solidarity among the group leaders claim to represent. This loyalty often translates into unwavering support for the leader or party, which can be mobilized quickly to drown out dissent or opposition. Political rallies, partisan media, and targeted propaganda are tools frequently used to reinforce in-group narratives and demonize out-group members.

## Manipulating Socio-Economic Anxieties

Exploitation of Economic Disparities: Economic anxieties are a fertile ground for division, especially in times of hardship or inequality. Politicians might exploit these anxieties by blaming economic problems on specific groups such as immigrants, minorities, or foreign nations rather than addressing the systemic issues at play. This scapegoating diverts attention from substantive economic policies and fosters a climate of resentment and competition among different societal segments.

The promise of Exclusive Benefits: To strengthen support, leaders may promise policies that purportedly benefit only their group at the expense of others. This can include tax cuts for certain income groups, protectionist policies to benefit local industries, or social programs designed for specific demographics. While these policies might provide short-term relief or gains for some, they often exacerbate long-term divisions and hinder comprehensive solutions that benefit society as a whole.

## Implications for Democracy and Social Cohesion

Erosion of Democratic Norms: The tactics of fear, division, and identity politics can significantly erode democratic norms. As politics becomes more about winning at all costs rather than governance, compromises become rare, and the political arena becomes a zero-sum game. This environment discourages cooperation between different political groups and undermines the collaborative spirit necessary for democracy.

Loss of Social Cohesion: The social fabric of the nation can be severely damaged by sustained divisions. Communities may become isolated, and mutual suspicion can replace social trust. In such a divided society, the concept of a common good diminishes, and collective action becomes challenging. This fragmentation can lead to a cycle of resentment and retaliation, which may manifest in social unrest or even violence.

## Counterstrategies and Building Bridges

Promoting Inclusive Politics: Counteracting the divisive use of fear and identity politics involves promoting an inclusive political discourse that emphasizes common goals and shared values. This includes policies and narratives that focus on unity, collective progress, and the mutual benefits of diversity.

Education and Awareness: Raising awareness about the manipulative use of fear and division in politics can help immunize the public against such tactics. Educational programs that focus on media literacy, critical thinking, and the importance of diversity can empower citizens to recognize and resist divisive strategies.

Civic Engagement and Dialogue: Encouraging broad civic engagement and fostering dialogue between different community groups can help rebuild trust and understanding. Initiatives that bring diverse groups together for discussions, community projects, or policy-making can bridge divides and restore faith in collective governance.

In Essence The strategic use of fear, division, and identity politics to consolidate power poses a significant threat to democratic principles and social cohesion. By understanding these tactics and their impacts, societies can better prepare to counteract them and work towards more inclusive, fair, and unified political and social systems.

## Control of Education: Efforts to Influence Educational Curricula and Restrict Academic Freedom

Education is a powerful tool in shaping societal values and perceptions, and it often becomes a battleground for ideological conflicts. Efforts to control or influence educational curricula and restrict academic freedom are not new but have seen a resurgence as political and ideological divisions deepen. These efforts aim to promote specific ideological agendas, often at the expense of critical thinking and academic integrity. This section explores the methods, motivations, and consequences of attempts to control education within various contexts.

### *Influencing Educational Curricula*

Curriculum Changes and Standardization: One of the most direct ways to influence education is through changes to the curriculum. This can involve the introduction of standardized tests that emphasize certain ideologies or viewpoints, revisions to textbooks to alter historical narratives or the omission of controversial topics. In some cases, states or local school boards push for curriculum changes that reflect a particular political or cultural perspective, which can lead to a homogenized educational experience that excludes diverse viewpoints.

Examples of Ideological Influence: For instance, debates over how topics like slavery, civil rights, or even climate change are taught in schools often reflect deeper ideological divides. Some conservative boards or lawmakers have pushed for "patriotic education" that emphasizes a positive view of national history, potentially glossing over complex or negative aspects. Conversely, there are movements to include more comprehensive discussions of systemic racism or environmental issues, which can be met with resistance from groups fearing ideological indoctrination.

## *Restricting Academic Freedom*

Legislation Against Academic Theories and Concepts: Recent efforts to restrict academic freedom have focused on legislation against teaching certain academic theories or concepts, particularly those related to race and gender. For example, several state legislatures have introduced bills that ban the teaching of Critical Race Theory, citing it as divisive or anti-American. These laws not only limit what educators can discuss but also discourage open academic inquiry.

Impact on Higher Education: In higher education, the push to control academic discourse extends to the monitoring or regulation of university courses, research funding, and public engagements by academics. Professors may face pressure or threats to their tenure and funding over research or lectures that are perceived as politically controversial. This environment can stifle innovation and critical scholarship, central components of higher education's mission.

## *Promotion of Alternative Educational Systems*

Support for Private and Charter Schools: Another strategy to influence education involves promoting alternative educational systems, such as private or charter schools, that are often less regulated in terms of curriculum. Supporters argue that these schools offer higher quality and more ideologically aligned education compared to public schools. However, this can also lead to a fragmented education system where children receive vastly different educations based on ideological lines.

Voucher Programs and School Choice Initiatives: Voucher programs and school choice initiatives are often touted as ways to give parents more control over their children's education by allowing public funding for private schooling. While proponents claim these programs promote educational excellence and competition, critics argue they can drain resources from public schools and lead to greater segregation and inequality in education.

## *Implications for Democracy and Society*

Erosion of Critical Thinking Skills: By restricting the scope of educational content and debate, efforts to control education can lead to an erosion of critical thinking skills among students. Education that prioritizes conformity over inquiry might produce citizens who are less able to engage critically with complex social and political issues.

Polarization and Social Division: When education becomes a tool for promoting specific ideologies, it can contribute to social and political polarization. Suppose young people are only exposed to one viewpoint. In that case, they may be less tolerant of differing perspectives, leading to social fragmentation.

Undermining Scientific and Intellectual Progress: Academic freedom is crucial for scientific and intellectual progress. Limiting this freedom can slow innovation and research, particularly in fields like science, technology, and humanities, which rely on the free exchange of ideas to advance knowledge.

## *Counteracting Educational Control*

Advocacy for Inclusive Curricula: Educators, parents, and civil society groups can play a key role in advocating for inclusive and balanced curricula that expose students to a range of perspectives. This can involve participating in school board meetings, curriculum reviews, and public discussions.

Support for Academic Freedom: The academic community and its allies must continue to defend academic freedom by resisting censorship and supporting targeted educators and researchers. This includes legal challenges to restrictive laws, public advocacy campaigns, and international support networks for scholars at risk.

Public Education Campaigns: Public education campaigns can raise awareness about the importance of a comprehensive education that fosters critical thinking and respect for diverse viewpoints. Such campaigns can help build public consensus against ideological control of education.

In Essence Efforts to control education and restrict academic freedom are deeply consequential for democratic societies. They not only shape how young people understand and engage with the world but also influence the broader political and cultural climate. A robust response that champions inclusive education and defends academic freedom is essential to ensuring that education remains a tool for empowerment rather than indoctrination, fostering a society that values critical inquiry and respects diverse perspectives.

# Chapter 6: Undermining Checks and Balances

# Executive Power Expansion: Analyzing the Republican Agenda's Impact on Government Balance

The expansion of executive power, particularly under Republican leadership, has raised significant concerns about the balance of power among the branches of the U.S. government. This trend involves consolidating authority within the executive branch at the expense of the legislative and judicial branches, potentially undermining the checks and balances that are foundational to American democracy. This section examines the methods and implications of this power shift, highlighting recent trends and specific instances where executive power has been expanded.

## *Tactics for Expanding Executive Power*

Use of Executive Orders and Actions: One of the primary tools for expanding executive power is the increased use of executive orders and other unilateral executive actions. These tools allow the President to bypass Congress on issues ranging from immigration policy to environmental regulations. While executive orders are a legitimate part of presidential power, their overuse can tip the balance of power away from the legislative branch, which is intended to be the primary body for making laws.

Emergency Declarations: Republican administrations have also used national emergency declarations to undertake actions that would normally require congressional approval. For example, national emergencies have been declared to deal with situations that arguably do not meet the typical criteria for such declarations, thereby allowing the executive to redirect funds and take other actions without the usual legislative oversight.

## *Undermining Legislative Authority*

Bypassing Congressional Oversight: The executive branch under Republican leadership has often sought to diminish the role of Congress in the governance process. This includes refusing to cooperate with congressional inquiries, withholding information necessary for legislative oversight, and declaring issues to be matters of executive privilege. Such actions not only undermine the legislative branch's ability to perform its constitutionally mandated oversight role but also shift the balance of power toward the executive.

Legislative Inaction and Gridlock: Expanding executive power has also been facilitated by legislative gridlock. When Congress is unable to pass legislation due to partisan divisions, the executive branch often steps in to fill the void through executive orders or administrative rule-making. While this can be seen as a response to legislative inaction, it also encourages a long-term shift in power dynamics by normalizing the executive's role as a primary policy-maker.

## *Limiting Judicial Oversight*

Appointing Partisan Judges: A key strategy for expanding executive power involves shaping the judiciary to be more favorable to the executive's agenda. This is accomplished by appointing judges who are ideologically aligned with the executive branch. Over time, this can lead to a judiciary that is less likely to check executive overreach and more likely to uphold executive actions, even those that might push the boundaries of legal authority.

Challenging Judicial Independence: Executive challenges to judicial decisions and authority also reflect an attempt to weaken the judiciary's role as a check on executive power. This includes publicly criticizing judges or judicial decisions that are unfavorable to the executive branch, which can undermine public confidence in the judicial system.

## *Implications for Democratic Governance*

Erosion of Checks and Balances: The concentration of power in the executive branch disrupts the balance of power established by the U.S. Constitution. This erosion of checks and balances can lead to executive overreach and a weakened legislative and judicial capacity to hold the executive accountable.

Impact on Civil Liberties and Rights: An empowered executive can pose risks to civil liberties and individual rights, especially if the expansion of power includes actions that bypass legal or legislative scrutiny. This might include surveillance, detention, and other measures that infringe on personal freedoms.

Long-term Institutional Changes: The shift in power dynamics can lead to long-term changes in how government functions, potentially embedding a stronger executive role into the fabric of U.S. governance. This could alter the effectiveness of democratic institutions and reduce the ability of future administrations to govern without excessive reliance on executive powers.

## *Strategies for Restoring Balance*

Legislative Reassertion: Congress can take steps to reclaim its legislative authority by limiting the scope of executive orders, strengthening oversight mechanisms, and being more proactive in the legislative process. This includes passing laws that explicitly limit the executive's unilateral powers and improving the transparency and accountability measures that govern executive actions.

Judicial Independence: Protecting the independence of the judiciary is crucial for maintaining checks on executive power. This involves ensuring that judicial appointments are made based on qualifications and respect for judicial independence rather than ideological alignment with the executive branch.

Public Awareness and Engagement: Encouraging public awareness of and engagement with issues related to the separation of powers can help hold leaders accountable. An informed and active citizenry is essential for pushing back against the expansion of executive power and advocating for a balanced government structure.

In Essence The expansion of executive power under Republican administrations poses significant challenges to the principles of separation of powers and checks and balances that underpin American democracy. By consolidating authority and diminishing the roles of the legislative and judicial branches, these trends threaten the democratic process and the protection of individual rights. Addressing this issue requires concerted efforts from all branches of government and the public to ensure that power remains balanced and that democratic institutions can function as intended.

## Weakening Congressional Oversight: Diminishing the Role

## of Congress in Checking Executive Actions

Congressional oversight is a critical function in the U.S. government, serving as a key mechanism to check and balance the powers of the Executive Branch. However, recent trends have shown a concerted effort to diminish the effectiveness of this oversight, particularly under administrations that seek to expand executive power. This erosion of congressional authority not only disrupts the balance of power established by the U.S. Constitution but also poses significant risks to democratic governance. This section explores the methods by which congressional oversight has been weakened, the motivations behind these efforts, and the potential consequences for American democracy.

### *Strategies to Undermine Congressional Oversight*

Non-Compliance with Congressional Subpoenas: One of the most direct methods of weakening congressional oversight is the executive branch's refusal to comply with congressional subpoenas. By not providing documents or preventing officials from testifying, the executive can obstruct Congress's ability to conduct thorough investigations into government operations or potential misconduct. This tactic has been employed in various contexts, from inquiries into national security matters to investigations of alleged corruption or abuse of power within the executive branch.

Claiming Executive Privilege: The use of executive privilege to withhold information is another strategy that has been increasingly utilized. While executive privilege is a legitimate executive power meant to protect sensitive information, its overuse or misuse can serve to block congressional access to critical data necessary for effective oversight. This tactic can significantly hinder investigations, especially those related to the president's conduct or decisions.

### *Legislative Inaction and Partisan Divides*

Partisan Gridlock: Partisan divisions within Congress can also undermine oversight by leading to inconsistent or selective scrutiny of the executive. When the president's party controls one or both chambers of Congress, there may be less motivation to investigate or challenge the executive branch rigorously.

This partisanship can result in weakened oversight, as majority parties often prioritize political loyalty over the congressional duty to check the executive.

Lack of Legislative Willpower: Even beyond partisanship, there is often a lack of willpower among lawmakers to assert their oversight responsibilities. This can be due to political pressure, lack of resources, or the complexities of mobilizing a coordinated response among a large and diverse body. When Congress fails to act decisively or to use the tools at its disposal effectively, it cedes power to the executive and diminishes its role in governance.

## Impact on the Balance of Power and Governance

Erosion of Checks and Balances: The weakening of congressional oversight leads directly to an erosion of the checks and balances that are foundational to American democracy. Without robust oversight, the executive branch can operate with increased autonomy and less accountability, potentially leading to excesses or abuses of power that remain unchecked and unresolved.

Policy Implications: A lack of effective oversight can also have significant policy implications. For instance, without adequate scrutiny, executive policies related to national security, foreign affairs, environmental regulation, and other critical areas may not reflect the broader public interest or may be implemented without sufficient consideration of their broader impacts.

## Consequences for Public Trust and Democratic Health

Decline in Public Trust: Public trust in government can significantly decline when it appears that the executive operates without sufficient oversight. This perception can lead to cynicism about the political process, alienation from government institutions, and a reduced likelihood of civic engagement among the populace.

Vulnerability to Corruption and Mismanagement: Reduced oversight can increase the vulnerability of government to corruption, mismanagement, and inefficiency. When there are no effective checks on executive power, there is a higher risk that decisions are made based on personal or political interests rather than the public good.

## *Strategies to Strengthen Congressional Oversight*

Enhanced Legal Mechanisms: To counteract these trends, Congress can strengthen legal mechanisms to enforce subpoenas and ensure compliance with oversight duties. This might include reforms to streamline the process of enforcing congressional subpoenas or new legislation to penalize non-compliance more effectively.

Bipartisan Cooperation: Enhancing bipartisan cooperation on oversight matters can help reduce the impact of partisanship on the oversight process. Establishing bipartisan committees or task forces to oversee critical areas can help ensure that oversight duties are carried out effectively regardless of which party controls Congress or the White House.

Public Engagement and Awareness: Increasing public awareness of the importance of congressional oversight can also play a crucial role. By educating the public about the risks of weakened oversight and mobilizing constituents to demand greater accountability, lawmakers can be pressured to take their oversight responsibilities more seriously.

In Essence, The weakening of congressional oversight represents a significant challenge to the integrity and effectiveness of American governance. By understanding the methods, motivations, and consequences associated with these efforts, stakeholders can work towards solutions that reinforce the checks and balances essential for a healthy democracy. Strengthening oversight is not only about maintaining governmental balance but also about ensuring that the executive branch operates with transparency, accountability, and respect for democratic norms.

## Threats to State and Local Governance: Federal Overreach and Its Impact on Autonomy

Federalism is a cornerstone of the U.S. political system, designed to allocate power between federal and state governments to preserve local autonomy and prevent the concentration of centralized power. However, instances of federal overreach can undermine this balance, infringing on the rights and responsibilities of state and local governments. This overreach not only strains the relationship between different levels of government but also can stifle local innovation and responsiveness. This section explores how federal overreach manifests, its effects on state and local governance, and the broader implications for democracy.

## *Forms of Federal Overreach*

Preemption of State Laws: One common form of federal overreach is the preemption of state laws, where federal legislation or regulations invalidate state policies. While preemption is sometimes necessary for ensuring national standards, its excessive use can undermine state efforts to legislate according to local preferences and needs. For example, federal preemption in areas like environmental regulation and consumer protection often sparks controversy, particularly when it nullifies more stringent state laws designed to protect local environments or consumers.

Conditional Federal Funding: The federal government frequently uses the promise of federal funding to influence state policies. This practice can border on coercion. Through mechanisms like grants and aid programs, the federal government sets conditions that states must meet to receive funding. These conditions may require states to alter their policies or administration in ways that align with federal priorities, potentially sidelining local objectives or constraints.

## *Impact on State and Local Autonomy*

Eroding Local Control: Federal overreach can erode local control over issues that are traditionally managed at the state or local level, such as education, land use, and policing. When the federal government imposes one-size-fits-all solutions, it can disregard the unique cultural, economic, and geographical contexts of states and communities, leading to policies that are less effective or even counterproductive at the local level.

Limiting Policy Innovation: States are often referred to as "laboratories of democracy" because they can experiment with policies that might later be adopted at the national level. However, federal overreach can stifle this innovation by limiting states' ability to test new ideas. This is particularly detrimental in areas like health care, environmental protection, and economic development, where localized approaches are crucial for addressing specific regional challenges.

## *Strained Intergovernmental Relations*

Legal Conflicts: Increased federal overreach often leads to legal conflicts between state and federal governments. States may challenge federal mandates or regulations through lawsuits, claiming that they infringe on states' rights as outlined in the Constitution. These legal battles can strain intergovernmental relations and lead to a contentious and adversarial atmosphere that hampers cooperative efforts.

Political Tensions: Political tensions can escalate when state and local leaders feel federal actions are undermining their authority. Such tensions may not only affect the specific areas of policy involved but also spill over into other aspects of intergovernmental cooperation, making it difficult to collaborate even on non-controversial issues.

## *Broader Implications for Governance*

Decreased Public Trust: When local governments are unable to enforce policies that reflect the preferences of their constituents due to federal overreach, it can lead to decreased public trust in all levels of government. Citizens may feel that their votes and voices matter less if local leaders are perceived as powerless against federal mandates.

Reduced Responsiveness to Local Needs: Local governments are typically more attuned to the specific needs and issues of their communities. Federal overreach can reduce the responsiveness of policies, as decisions made at the national level may not accurately reflect local realities. This disconnect can result in inefficient use of resources and policies that fail to address or even exacerbate, local problems.

## *Strategies for Balancing Federal and Local Interests*

Advocacy and Lobbying: State and local governments can engage in more robust advocacy and lobbying efforts to influence federal policies and protect their interests. By forming coalitions or working through intergovernmental organizations, they can present a united front that amplifies their influence in federal decision-making processes.

Legal Safeguards: Strengthening legal safeguards that protect state rights can help prevent undue federal interference. This might involve pushing for clearer definitions of federal and state powers in legislation or seeking constitutional protections that reinforce federalism.

Public Engagement: Encouraging public engagement in governance can help ensure that federal policies reflect local needs and preferences. By mobilizing constituents to voice their opinions on federal actions that affect local governance, state and local leaders can bolster their position in negotiations with federal authorities.

In Essence Federal overreach poses significant threats to the autonomy of state and local governments, undermining the principles of federalism that underpin the U.S. political system. By eroding local control, stifling innovation, and straining intergovernmental relations, excessive federal interference can diminish the effectiveness and responsiveness of governance at all levels. Addressing these challenges requires a concerted effort from state and local governments to assert their rights, engage with federal policymakers, and encourage public participation in the democratic process.

# Chapter 7: The Road to Dictatorship

## Current Trends: Indications of a Move Towards Authoritarian Rule

In recent years, there has been a discernible shift in various parts of the world, including some democratic nations, towards policies and actions that bear the hallmarks of authoritarian rule. This trend is characterized by the centralization of power, erosion of checks and balances, suppression of dissent, and weakening of democratic institutions. This section examines present-day actions and policies that suggest a global and domestic move towards authoritarian governance, highlighting the key areas of concern and the implications for democracy.

### *Consolidation of Executive Power*

Expanding Executive Authority: A significant trend in authoritarian drift is the expansion of executive power at the expense of legislative and judicial oversight. Leaders in various countries have taken steps to extend their terms through constitutional amendments or have bypassed parliaments with emergency decrees that grant sweeping powers to the executive branch.

Weakening Legislative Bodies: In some cases, legislative bodies have been stripped of their powers, their roles largely reduced to rubber-stamping executive decisions. This erosion of legislative power undermines the principle of separation of powers. It leads to a concentration of authority, which is a key feature of authoritarian rule.

### *Undermining Judicial Independence*

Stacking Courts: The independence of the judiciary has been threatened by leaders appointing judges who are loyal to them rather than those who are impartial. This politicization of the judiciary compromises its role as a check on executive power. It can lead to unjust legal rulings that support the interests of the ruling elite.

Attacking Judicial Decisions: There has also been an increase in public attacks on judges and their decisions, particularly when they are unfavorable to the government. This not only undermines the credibility of the judiciary but also erodes public trust in the legal system as a fair arbitrator of disputes.

## Restricting Freedoms and Civil Liberties

Suppressing Free Speech and Media: Authoritarian trends include significant restrictions on freedom of speech and press. Governments have enacted laws that criminalize dissent, label criticism as disinformation, or broadly define terrorism in ways that include peaceful protest. Media outlets that criticize the government face harassment, censorship, or closure, reducing the diversity of viewpoints and controlling the public narrative.

Surveillance and Privacy Invasions: Increased surveillance measures, often justified on national security grounds, have led to significant invasions of privacy. These measures provide governments with the ability to closely monitor and sometimes manipulate citizen behavior, stifling opposition and curbing democratic freedoms.

## Manipulating Electoral Processes

Eroding Electoral Integrity: There is growing concern over the integrity of elections in several countries. Tactics include gerrymandering, voter suppression, manipulation of electoral boundaries, and the disenfranchisement of opposition groups. Such manipulations ensure power remains with the current leadership, diminishing the public's ability to change their rulers through democratic means.

Politicization of Electoral Bodies: Electoral commissions and other bodies that oversee elections are increasingly being staffed by partisan figures, compromising their neutrality and ability to conduct fair elections. This trend is alarming as it directly threatens the democratic process.

## Cultivating a Personality Cult

Promotion of Personalist Rule: In many authoritarian regimes, there is a noticeable shift towards personalist rule, where the political identity of the country becomes closely tied to a single leader. These leaders often cultivate a personality cult, emphasizing their unique ability to govern and solve the nation's problems, which can justify their continued hold on power.

### *International Implications and Responses*

Global Democratic Backsliding: The trend towards authoritarianism is not confined to any one region but is part of a global pattern of democratic backsliding. This raises concerns about the future of international norms and agreements that depend on democratic governance and mutual respect for democratic values.

International Actions and Sanctions: In response to these trends, international bodies and some nations have imposed sanctions or taken other actions against regimes that are perceived as moving towards authoritarian rule. However, the effectiveness of these measures is still subject to debate, as geopolitical interests often dilute the willingness to act decisively.

In Essence, The move towards authoritarian rule in various contexts poses a significant challenge to the principles of democratic governance. This trend is characterized by the consolidation of power, undermining of democratic institutions, restriction of civil liberties, and manipulation of electoral processes. Domestic and international actors must recognize and address these trends proactively to safeguard democratic values and promote a governance structure that respects freedom, fairness, and the rule of law.

## Future Scenarios: Potential Outcomes of Continued Authoritarian Trends

The global shift towards authoritarian practices has significant implications for the future of governance, both in individual nations and internationally. If current trends continue, the erosion of democratic norms could lead to a range of severe political environments, from entrenched one-party states to outright dictatorships. This section speculates on potential future scenarios under such trajectories, examining their likely impacts on societal structure, global stability, and human rights.

### *Establishment of One-Party States*

Political Monopoly: In scenarios where one party consolidates significant power, we might see the formal or de facto establishment of one-party states. These states may maintain the facade of democratic processes, such as elections. Still, these processes could be so manipulated or controlled that true competition is impossible. Political opposition might be either legally prohibited or so severely curtailed that it cannot effectively challenge the ruling party.

Implications for Governance: The governance in a one-party state typically lacks transparency and accountability. Corruption may become rampant, as the lack of opposition allows the ruling party to operate with little oversight. Policy-making might favor the interests of party elites or their allies, leading to uneven economic development and increased inequality.

## *Transition to Outright Dictatorships*

Concentration of Power: If the centralization of power continues unchecked, some countries might transition from authoritarian regimes to full dictatorships. This shift could occur through gradual changes, such as the elimination of term limits and the suppression of all opposition, or through more abrupt means, such as a coup by the ruling party or leader.

Societal Control: In a dictatorship, the personal whims of the dictator could dictate policy, and the rule of man might entirely supplant the rule of law. The state might employ extensive surveillance and harsh penalties to quash dissent, leading to a climate of fear and repression.

## *Erosion of Civil Liberties and Human Rights*

Suppression of Freedom: Under both one-party states and dictatorships, civil liberties such as freedom of speech, assembly, and the press are likely to be heavily restricted. The state might justify such measures as necessary for national security or the preservation of order. Still, the true aim would be to prevent challenges to the regime.

Human Rights Violations: With the erosion of accountability mechanisms, human rights violations could become both more frequent and more severe.

These might include arbitrary detention, torture, and other abuses that are often associated with authoritarian regimes.

## *Economic and Social Implications*

Economic Instability: The concentration of political power can lead to economic policies that favor elites, stifling innovation and leading to economic inefficiencies. Over time, this might result in economic instability and diminished prosperity for the general population.

Social Fragmentation: The systemic exclusion of certain groups from power under authoritarian regimes can exacerbate social divisions and lead to conflict. In extreme cases, this could result in civil unrest or even civil war, particularly if large segments of the population become disenfranchised.

## *Global Impact and International Relations*

Isolation or Alliance Formation: Authoritarian states might find themselves increasingly isolated on the global stage, particularly if their human rights records become egregious. Alternatively, they might form alliances with other authoritarian regimes, potentially leading to a bloc of states that challenge international norms and promote authoritarian governance.

Impact on Global Stability: The rise of authoritarianism can lead to increased global instability. Authoritarian leaders might engage in aggressive foreign policies to divert attention from domestic issues, leading to conflicts or international crises.

## *Potential for Democratic Resurgence*

Resistance and Reform: Even in authoritarian regimes, there is potential for resistance and reform. Public dissatisfaction with governance failures and systemic abuses can lead to grassroots movements, uprisings, or reform-oriented factions within the government advocating for change.

International Support and Intervention: The international community could play a crucial role in supporting democratic movements within authoritarian states through diplomatic pressure, sanctions, or support for civil society.

In Essence If current trends toward authoritarianism continue, the potential scenarios range from the establishment of one-party states to outright dictatorships. These scenarios pose significant risks to civil liberties, economic stability, and global peace. However, the future is not predetermined, and actions taken by citizens, governments, and international bodies can influence these outcomes. The resilience of democratic institutions and the spirit of global cooperation will be critical in confronting these authoritarian trends and promoting more inclusive and accountable governance.

## Global Comparisons: The U.S. Situation and Transitions from Democracy to Dictatorship

The transition from democracy to dictatorship has occurred in various regions across the globe, offering valuable lessons and warnings about the risks and mechanisms that facilitate such transformations. While the United States has a robust democratic tradition, examining the paths other nations have taken toward authoritarianism can provide critical insights. This comparison not only highlights potential vulnerabilities but also underscores the steps necessary to safeguard democratic institutions.

### *Mechanisms of Democratic Erosion*

Erosion of Checks and Balances: In many countries that have transitioned to authoritarian rule, a common early sign was the erosion of checks and balances. Leaders often sought to consolidate power by weakening the judiciary and legislative branches, much like concerns currently seen in the U.S. For instance, Turkey under Recep Tayyip ErdoÄŸan has seen significant curtailment of judicial independence and legislative power, centralizing authority in the executive.

Suppression of Media and Free Speech: Countries like Venezuela under Hugo ChÃ¡vez and NicolÃ¡s Maduro have demonstrated how the suppression of media and free speech can be instrumental in a democratic to authoritarian transition. By controlling information and limiting free expression, these leaders have stifled opposition and maintained power despite economic and social turmoil.

## Use of Populism and Nationalism

Populism as a Tool: Populism has often been a precursor to authoritarianism, as leaders use it to appeal directly to the masses while bypassing traditional democratic institutions. The U.S. has seen similar trends, with populist rhetoric becoming a prominent feature of political discourse, focusing on anti-elite sentiments that sometimes overshadow reasoned policy debate.

Exploiting Nationalism: Leaders like Viktor OrbÃ¡n in Hungary have used nationalism to fortify their rule by promoting a unified national identity that often excludes minorities and opposition groups. This tactic has parallels in the U.S., where nationalistic rhetoric has sometimes been used to marginalize groups and consolidate a base of support around cultural and identity politics.

## Manipulation of Electoral Systems

Undermining Electoral Integrity: In Russia, Vladimir Putin has maintained power through various means, including the manipulation of electoral systems to ensure favorable outcomes. Similar concerns have been raised in the U.S., where allegations of voter suppression and gerrymandering persist, posing threats to the integrity of elections.

Politicization of Electoral Institutions: Countries like Poland have seen the politicization of electoral institutions, which undermines public trust in electoral processes. Comparatively, in the U.S., debates over the role and impartiality of electoral oversight bodies have intensified, reflecting concerns over their ability to function without political interference.

## Judicial Takeover and Legal Manipulation

Appointment of Sympathetic Judges: Just as Turkey and Venezuela have seen the appointment of pro-government judges to key judicial positions, the U.S.

has experienced contentious and highly politicized Supreme Court appointments that have raised concerns about the long-term impartiality of the judiciary.

Use of Law to Suppress Opposition: In Egypt, under Abdel Fattah el-Sisi, laws have been tailored to criminalize opposition and restrict civil society. The U.S. faces its challenges with legal frameworks being leveraged to challenge the legitimacy of political opposition, though to a less extreme extent.

## *International Context and Response*

International Isolation vs. Engagement: Countries transitioning to dictatorship often face international isolation. However, some manage to maintain strategic alliances that support their authoritarian regimes. The U.S. is in a unique position with its strong historical ties to democratic nations. However, its international standing can be compromised if democratic norms continue to erode.

Global Democratic Recession: The trend towards authoritarianism is not limited to isolated cases but is part of a broader global democratic recession. The U.S., traditionally a promoter of democracy, finds its democratic norms under scrutiny, impacting its ability to lead globally on these issues.

In Essence The transition from democracy to dictatorship in various countries offers critical lessons for the United States. By understanding the mechanisms that facilitate such transitions, such as the erosion of checks and balances, suppression of dissent, and manipulation of electoral processes, the U.S. can take proactive steps to safeguard its democracy. Vigilance, robust public engagement, and a recommitment to democratic principles are essential to prevent a similar trajectory and ensure the resilience of democratic institutions.

# Chapter 8: Defending Democracy

# Grassroots Movements: Their Role in Resisting Authoritarian Tendencies

Grassroots movements have historically played a crucial role in resisting authoritarian tendencies and promoting democratic principles. These movements, driven by community-level activism and popular engagement, are often at the forefront of efforts to defend civil liberties, human rights, and democratic governance. Their influence spans across various spheres, including political, social, and environmental domains, demonstrating a versatile and effective approach to activism. This section explores the significance of grassroots organizations in countering authoritarianism, their strategies, and the challenges they face.

## Mobilizing Public Opinion

Awareness and Education: Grassroots organizations often focus on raising awareness and educating the public about the signs and dangers of authoritarian rule. By disseminating information through community meetings, workshops, and social media, these movements help people understand their rights and the importance of democratic institutions. This educational role is crucial in environments where mainstream media may be restricted or biased.

Amplifying Voices: These organizations excel at amplifying the voices of marginalized or oppressed groups whose concerns might be ignored or suppressed in authoritarian regimes. By bringing these voices to the forefront, grassroots movements foster a more inclusive dialogue that challenges the exclusionary narratives often favored by authoritarian leaders.

## Organizing and Mobilizing

Protests and Demonstrations: Grassroots movements are pivotal in organizing protests, demonstrations, and other forms of public dissent that draw attention to authoritarian practices and demand change. These public displays of resistance can significantly impact public opinion and political decision-making, providing a visible counterforce to authoritarian actions.

Building Networks: By building networks of activists, volunteers, and sympathetic organizations, grassroots movements create a robust infrastructure capable of coordinated action. These networks are essential for mobilizing resources, sharing information quickly, and sustaining long-term resistance against authoritarian tendencies.

## Advocating for Policy Change

Legislative Advocacy: Grassroots movements often engage in direct advocacy, pushing for legislative changes that protect democratic processes and promote transparency and accountability in government. By lobbying lawmakers and participating in public hearings, they influence policy at both local and national levels.

Legal Challenges: Many grassroots organizations work with legal experts to challenge authoritarian policies in court. Through strategic litigation, they can achieve significant victories that uphold constitutional rights and set important legal precedents.

## International Collaboration and Solidarity

Global Networks: Grassroots movements increasingly operate within global networks, collaborating with international NGOs, advocacy groups, and civil society organizations. These connections enhance their ability to learn from global best practices, gain international support, and apply pressure through global advocacy platforms.

Solidarity Campaigns: International solidarity campaigns can draw global attention to local issues, putting pressure on authoritarian regimes from abroad and providing moral and material support to local activists. This international dimension can be crucial in cases where domestic avenues for resistance are heavily suppressed.

## Challenges Facing Grassroots Movements

Suppression by the State: Authoritarian regimes often target grassroots movements through surveillance, harassment, and legal actions designed to intimidate activists and disrupt their activities. Such repressive measures continually test the resilience and adaptability of these movements.

Resource Limitations: Grassroots organizations frequently operate with limited resources, relying heavily on volunteer efforts and small-scale donations. Sustaining long-term campaigns under such conditions is challenging, especially when facing the extensive resources of an authoritarian state.

## *Impact and Importance*

Catalysts for Democratic Renewal: Grassroots movements have repeatedly proven to be catalysts for democratic renewal. Their ability to engage and mobilize ordinary citizens plays a critical role in revitalizing democratic practices and restoring public faith in democratic institutions.

Guardians of Democracy: By standing as vigilant guardians of democracy, these movements not only resist authoritarian encroachments but also foster a culture of active citizenship and participation that is fundamental to a healthy democracy.

In Essence Grassroots movements are indispensable in the fight against authoritarian tendencies. Through their efforts to educate, mobilize, and advocate, they play a pivotal role in sustaining democratic norms and challenging repressive actions. Despite facing significant challenges, the resilience and dedication of grassroots activists continue to inspire democratic engagement and hope for a more accountable and inclusive governance system. The success of these movements often signals the health and vibrancy of democracy itself, underscoring the need for continued support and recognition of their critical role in society.

## Legal and Institutional Safeguards: Protecting Democracy through Reform and Regulation

To safeguard democracy against authoritarian tendencies, legal actions and institutional reforms play a crucial role. These measures are designed to strengthen the rule of law, ensure transparency, and maintain a healthy balance of power among governmental branches. This section explores key legal and institutional strategies that can be employed to protect democratic processes and principles.

## Strengthening Legal Frameworks

Constitutional Safeguards: Reviewing and amending the constitution to include clearer safeguards against the abuse of power is fundamental. This could involve setting stricter limits on executive powers, enhancing protections for civil liberties, and defining more explicitly the checks and balances among branches of government.

Anti-Corruption Legislation: Implementing robust anti-corruption laws is essential to prevent and penalize corruption within government institutions. These laws should be accompanied by strong enforcement mechanisms and independent oversight bodies, such as anti-corruption commissions, which operate free from political interference.

## Ensuring Judicial Independence

Judicial Appointments: Reforming the judicial appointment process to ensure it is transparent, merit-based, and insulated from political pressures is crucial for maintaining an impartial judiciary. Establishing independent judicial selection commissions can help achieve this by vetting candidates based on professional qualifications rather than political loyalty.

Protection from Political Retaliation: Implementing legal protections for judges from political retaliation is necessary to safeguard judicial independence. This could include laws that make it harder to impeach judges without substantial evidence of wrongdoing or misconduct.

## Reforming Electoral Systems

Voting Rights Protections: Strengthening voting rights through legislation that ensures all citizens have fair and equal access to voting is critical. This includes measures to prevent gerrymandering, eliminate discriminatory voting laws, and expand voting access through means such as early voting and mail-in ballots.

Election Oversight: Enhancing the independence and capabilities of electoral oversight bodies to conduct free and fair elections is another vital safeguard. This includes ensuring these bodies have the authority and resources to oversee elections effectively, from the campaigning phase to the final count of votes.

## Promoting Transparency and Accountability

Freedom of Information Laws: Robust freedom of information laws enable citizens and the media to access government records, promoting transparency and accountability. Ensuring that these laws are enforced and that exceptions are narrowly tailored can prevent governments from operating in secrecy.

Whistleblower Protections: Enacting strong whistleblower protection laws encourages individuals within government or private sectors to report wrongdoing without fear of retaliation. These protections are essential for uncovering abuses of power and corruption.

## Decentralizing Power

Local Governance: Strengthening local governance by decentralizing powers can help counteract the over-concentration of power at higher levels of government. Providing local governments with greater autonomy and resources to address community-specific issues can enhance democratic participation and responsiveness.

Checks on Executive Power: Introducing legal limits on the use of executive orders and emergency powers can prevent the executive from bypassing the legislative process. This might include requirements for legislative approval to extend or renew emergency powers beyond a certain period.

## Civic Engagement and Public Education

Civic Education: Programs that educate citizens about their democratic rights and responsibilities can empower individuals to participate more actively in the political process. Civic education should be integrated into school curriculums and public campaigns to build a strong foundation for democratic engagement.

Public Participation in Governance: Creating mechanisms for greater public participation in decision-making processes, such as public referenda, community councils, and public hearings, can enhance democratic governance and ensure that government actions reflect the will of the people.

## *International Standards and Cooperation*

Adherence to International Norms: Committing to and implementing international human rights norms and democratic standards can provide an additional layer of protection for democracy. Participation in international bodies and adherence to their conventions can also provide benchmarks and external accountability for democratic practices.

International Monitoring and Support: International organizations can play a supportive role in monitoring elections, assessing human rights practices, and providing technical assistance to strengthen democratic institutions. This international involvement can help to legitimize and reinforce domestic efforts to safeguard democracy.

In Essence Legal actions and institutional reforms are critical to protecting and sustaining democratic governance. By implementing comprehensive safeguards that enhance transparency, accountability, and participation, societies can fortify themselves against authoritarian encroachments. These efforts require continuous commitment and vigilance from all sectors of society to ensure that democracy not only survives but thrives.

## The Role of Citizens: Civic Engagement, Voting, and Public Participation in Safeguarding Democracy

In a democratic system, the role of citizens is paramount. Civic engagement, voting, and public participation form the bedrock of a healthy democracy, ensuring that the government remains responsive and accountable to the will of the people. Active participation by citizens helps to prevent the erosion of democratic norms. It serves as a vital check on the powers of elected officials. This section explores the importance of these activities and their impact on maintaining and strengthening democratic institutions.

### *Civic Engagement: Beyond Voting*

Informed Participation: Civic engagement involves staying informed about public issues and understanding the workings of government and political mechanisms. This knowledge empowers citizens to participate effectively in public debates and to hold public officials accountable. Educational initiatives and public awareness campaigns play crucial roles in fostering a well-informed citizenry.

Volunteering and Activism: Engaging in community service, joining local or national advocacy groups, or participating in issue-based activism can significantly impact societal change. These activities allow individuals to work collaboratively on common goals and influence policy decisions at various levels of government.

### *Voting: The Fundamental Act of Democracy*

Voter Participation: Voting is the most fundamental aspect of civic engagement in a democracy. It is the primary means through which citizens exercise their democratic right to choose their representatives. High voter turnout reflects a robust democratic engagement and legitimizes the electoral process and its outcomes.

Overcoming Barriers to Voting: Ensuring that all eligible citizens can vote without undue hardship is crucial. This includes combating voter suppression tactics, simplifying the voting process, expanding access through measures like early voting and mail-in ballots, and educating voters on their rights and the voting process.

### *Public Participation in Governance*

Engagement in Policy-making: Citizens can participate in governance not only by voting but also by attending town hall meetings public hearings, and serving on local advisory boards. Such participation ensures that diverse viewpoints are considered in governmental decision-making and that policies reflect the community's needs and aspirations.

Feedback Mechanisms: Establishing robust mechanisms for public feedback helps governments be more responsive to the needs of their constituents. This can include opinion surveys, public comment periods on upcoming legislation, and accessible communication channels with elected officials.

## Accountability and Transparency

Monitoring Government Actions: Citizens play a critical role in monitoring the actions of their government, ensuring transparency and accountability. This can be achieved through watchdog groups, independent media, and transparency initiatives that scrutinize government activities and expose corruption or maladministration.

Demanding Accountability: When officials fail to live up to their responsibilities, it is up to citizens to demand accountability, whether through peaceful protests, legal action, or voting them out of office. Active and persistent demands for accountability discourage potential abuses of power.

## Empowering Marginalized Voices

Inclusivity in Participation: Democracy is strengthened when it includes the voices of all segments of society, including those historically marginalized or underserved. Efforts to empower these groups to participate in political processes are vital to ensuring a truly representative democracy.

Community Representation: Ensuring that every community has representation in political processes helps to address unique challenges and bring diverse perspectives to the table, enhancing the deliberative process and fostering greater equity.

## The Role of Digital Tools in Enhancing Engagement

Leveraging Technology: Digital tools can enhance civic engagement by providing more accessible information about political processes and facilitating easier communication with representatives. Social media, online forums, and digital voting systems can extend the reach and efficiency of civic participation.

Countering Misinformation: Citizens must also be vigilant about the accuracy of information circulated online. Promoting media literacy and critical thinking is essential in combating misinformation, which can skew public perception and influence democratic outcomes.

In Essence The health of a democracy depends significantly on the active participation of its citizens. Civic engagement, voting, and public participation are not just rights but responsibilities that each citizen must embrace to safeguard their democratic institutions. Through informed and active involvement, citizens ensure that democracy in their country is not just a form of government but a continuous, participatory process that reflects the will and protects the rights of all people.

# Summary of Key Points: Recap of Main Arguments

Throughout this discussion, we've explored various facets of contemporary political dynamics, focusing on the challenges and threats to democracy, the roles and responsibilities of different stakeholders, and the mechanisms through which democratic principles can be upheld or undermined. Here is a recap of the main arguments made, distilled into key themes that highlight the ongoing struggle for democratic integrity.

## *Authoritarian Tendencies and Democratic Erosion*

Expansion of Executive Power: There has been a notable trend towards the expansion of executive authority at the expense of legislative and judicial checks, raising concerns about the balance of power within government.

Weakening of Congressional Oversight: Efforts to diminish the role of Congress in overseeing executive actions have weakened one of the fundamental checks and balances essential for democratic governance.

Threats to State and Local Autonomy: Federal overreach has increasingly encroached on the autonomy of state and local governments, challenging the federalist structure that supports diverse local governance.

## *The Role of Information and Media*

Misinformation and Propaganda: The manipulation of information through misinformation, conspiracy theories, and state-backed propaganda poses significant risks to informed public discourse and the healthy functioning of democracy.

Media Suppression and Control: Authoritarian regimes often seek to control or suppress the media to stifle opposition and maintain power, severely impacting the public's ability to make informed decisions.

## *Legal and Institutional Safeguards*

Judicial Independence: Upholding the independence of the judiciary is crucial for ensuring that laws are applied fairly and government actions are held accountable.

Electoral Integrity: Protecting the integrity of electoral processes is fundamental to ensuring that elections are free, fair, and reflect the true will of the people.

Anti-Corruption Measures: Robust legal frameworks to combat corruption are necessary to maintain trust in public institutions and ensure that they serve the public interest.

## Civic Engagement and Public Participation

Importance of Civic Participation: Active participation by citizens in political processes is crucial for maintaining a vibrant democracy. From voting to public demonstrations,

Empowerment of Marginalized Groups: Ensuring that all segments of society, especially marginalized groups, have the opportunity to participate in politics is essential for a truly representative democracy.

## Global Trends and Comparisons

Comparative Analysis: Examining other countries that have experienced democratic erosion or transitioned to authoritarian rule offers valuable lessons on the signs and consequences of such shifts.

International Support for Democracy: The role of international organizations and alliances in supporting democratic norms and practices can be a critical counterbalance to authoritarian tendencies.

## Future Scenarios and Preventative Strategies

Potential Outcomes: If current trends towards authoritarianism continue, the future could see more entrenched one-party states or outright dictatorships, with severe consequences for global stability and individual freedoms.

Strategies for Resistance: Strengthening democratic institutions, enhancing public engagement, and fostering international cooperation are essential strategies to resist authoritarianism and support democratic governance.

In Essence The arguments presented underscore the complex interplay between power, governance, and citizenry in shaping the landscape of modern democracies. By understanding these dynamics and actively participating in the democratic process, individuals and societies can work towards ensuring that their governments remain responsive, accountable, and truly democratic. The lessons drawn from global experiences and historical trends emphasize the need for vigilance and proactive engagement to safeguard the principles of freedom, equality, and justice.

# Call to Action: Defending Democracy and Resisting Authoritarianism

As we face the growing challenges of authoritarian tendencies and democratic erosion around the world, it is crucial for every citizen not only to be aware of these dangers but also to actively engage in defending democratic principles. The responsibility to safeguard democracy does not rest solely on the shoulders of politicians or leaders; it is a duty shared by all citizens. This call to action is a rallying cry for everyone to participate in the essential work of preserving and strengthening democracy.

### *Stay Informed and Educate Others*

Seek Reliable Information: Constantly seek out reliable, fact-based information sources to stay informed about local, national, and international political developments. A well-informed citizenry is the foundation of a robust democracy.

Educate Your Community: Share your knowledge with others. Organize or participate in educational workshops, discussion groups, or public lectures that help disseminate important information about democratic rights and responsibilities.

## Engage in Political Processes

Vote in All Elections: Exercise your right to vote in all local, state, and national elections. Your vote is a powerful tool in shaping the direction of your community and country.

Support Electoral Participation: Encourage others to register and vote. Participate in or organize voter registration drives and help remove barriers to voting in your community, such as offering transportation to polling stations or assisting with voter ID procurement.

## Hold Leaders Accountable

Demand Transparency and Accountability: Regularly communicate with your representatives and demand transparency and accountability in their actions. Attend town hall meetings, write letters, and call their offices to express your concerns and expectations.

Support Checks and Balances: Advocate for and support measures that strengthen checks and balances within government. This includes supporting independent judiciary systems, fair electoral processes, and effective legislative bodies.

## Participate in Civic Activities

Join or Support Civil Society Organizations: Engage with local or national groups that work on issues you care about, such as civil rights, environmental protection, or political reform. These organizations play a crucial role in mobilizing society to resist authoritarian moves and promote democratic governance.

Organize or Participate in Peaceful Protests: When necessary, participate in peaceful protests to oppose undemocratic actions and policies. Public demonstrations can be a powerful tool for signaling citizen discontent and solidarity.

## Promote Inclusivity and Dialogue

Foster Inclusive Communities: Work towards inclusivity in your community by bridging divides between different social, ethnic, or political groups. Inclusivity strengthens democracy by ensuring all voices are heard and valued.

Engage in Constructive Dialogue: Promote and engage in constructive dialogue with people who hold different views. Understanding and cooperation across political divides are essential for countering polarizing tendencies that can lead to authoritarianism.

## *Advocate for Policy Reforms*

Push for Democratic Reforms: Advocate for policy reforms that enhance democratic governance. This could include lobbying for campaign finance reform, anti-corruption measures, or laws that protect the freedom of the press.

Support International Efforts: Engage with and support international efforts that promote democracy globally. This can include participating in or supporting international watchdogs, human rights organizations, and other groups that monitor and challenge authoritarian practices worldwide.

In Essence Democracy is not autonomous; it requires the constant effort and vigilance of its citizens. By staying informed, engaging in political processes, holding leaders accountable, participating in civic activities, promoting inclusivity, and advocating for policy reforms, each individual can contribute to the defense of democracy. Now, more than ever, it is essential that we commit to these actions to ensure that democratic principles not only endure but thrive in the face of challenges. Let this be a call to action for all who value freedom and justice to stand up, speak out, and actively participate in the safeguarding of our democratic way of life.

## Hope for the Future: Returning to and Strengthening U.S. Democratic Institutions

Despite the challenges facing its democratic institutions, the United States holds a reservoir of civic spirit and constitutional principles that can guide a return to robust democracy. This vision for the future is grounded in a collective commitment to revitalizing democratic norms, enhancing transparency, and fostering a culture of civic engagement. By leveraging its foundational strengths and embracing necessary reforms, the U.S. can not only return to its democratic roots but also build a more resilient and inclusive democratic system.

## Reaffirming Democratic Commitments

Constitutional Renewal: Begin with a nationwide initiative to reaffirm the principles enshrined in the Constitution. This could involve educational campaigns, public discussions, and legislative reaffirmations that highlight the importance of checks and balances, the rule of law, and the rights of individuals.

Civic Education: Strengthen civic education in schools and communities to ensure that all citizens understand their rights and responsibilities. This education should emphasize critical thinking, the history of democratic institutions, and the importance of participation in democracy.

## Strengthening Electoral Integrity

Protecting Voter Rights: Implement comprehensive federal standards to protect voter rights, eliminate voter suppression, and ensure every citizen has equal access to the ballot box. This includes modernizing voting infrastructure to enhance accessibility and security.

Enhancing Representation: Consider reforms such as ranked-choice voting and the elimination of gerrymandering to ensure electoral processes are fair and truly representative. These changes can help reduce polarization and encourage more moderate and inclusive political discourse.

## Enhancing Transparency and Accountability

Government Transparency: Enact laws that increase transparency in government operations, campaign financing, and lobbying activities. This could involve stronger disclosure requirements and real-time transparency protocols.

Accountability Mechanisms: Strengthen the independence of bodies that oversee government accountability, such as inspectors general and ethics committees. Ensure these bodies are equipped with the necessary resources and legal authority to conduct effective oversight.

## Fostering Inclusive Governance

Diverse Representation: Promote policies that encourage diverse representation at all levels of government. This involves not only diversity in terms of race and gender but also in terms of economic background and professional experience.

Community Engagement Initiatives: Expand initiatives that encourage public participation in government decision-making. This could include town hall meetings, participatory budgeting, and advisory boards that allow citizens to contribute directly to policy decisions.

## Building Consensus and Bridging Divides

Bipartisan and Cross-Partisan Initiatives: Encourage the development of bipartisan and cross-partisan initiatives that aim to find common ground on critical issues facing the nation. These initiatives can help reduce the hyper-partisanship currently prevalent in political discourse.

Dialogue and Deliberation: Support platforms for dialogue and deliberation that allow citizens to engage with one another on contentious issues constructively and respectfully. Facilitated dialogue sessions and public deliberation forums can help bridge divides and foster a more cooperative political culture.

## Reforming Institutional Structures

Judicial and Legislative Reforms: Consider structural reforms that might include changes to the Supreme Court, such as term limits or an expansion in the number of justices, to reflect a broader range of perspectives and reduce political pressure on judicial decisions. In Congress, reforms might focus on rules that promote more collaborative legislation processes.

Decentralizing Power: Empower local governments by decentralizing power where appropriate, allowing for more tailored and responsive governance at the local level. This can help revitalize trust in government by bringing decision-making closer to the people.

## *Engaging with the Global Community*

International Democratic Standards: Reengage with international institutions that promote democratic standards and human rights. By playing a leading role in global democracy initiatives, the U.S. can reinforce its commitment to democratic principles both at home and abroad.

Support for Global Democracies: Actively support emerging democracies around the world through diplomacy, development aid, and cultural exchange programs. This not only helps stabilize global politics but also reinforces democratic norms within the U.S.

In Essence The path to revitalizing U.S. democracy is multifaceted, involving a commitment to foundational principles, structural reforms, and an engaged citizenry. By recommitting to the values of transparency, inclusivity, and accountability and by implementing strategic reforms, the United States can both return to its democratic roots and set a course for a stronger, more resilient democratic future. This vision is not only achievable but essential for the continued prosperity and stability of the nation and its people.

# Part II - Impact on the Priviledge White American

As the United States faces the potential drift toward authoritarianism, the consequences for various segments of the population can vary significantly. For Privileged White Americans, those who are typically more economically secure, socially influential, and with greater access to resources, the implications of such a shift can be complex and multifaceted. This section of the book delves into the nuanced ways in which moving toward an authoritarian regime under the guise of "The Republican Agenda: Undoing 200 Years of Democracy for a Dictatorship" could impact this demographic, highlighting both the potential short-term benefits they might experience and the significant long-term risks that could arise.

# Chapter 1: Short-Term Benefits

115

# Economic Gains: Short-Term Benefits for Privileged White Americans Under Authoritarian Shifts

In a political landscape that veers toward authoritarianism, policies that disproportionately benefit the wealthy often become prioritized. For Privileged White Americans, this shift can translate into significant economic advantages, at least in the short term. This section explores how tax cuts for the rich, deregulation of industries, and reduced corporate oversight could positively impact their financial status and business operations while also considering the broader implications of such policies.

## *Tax Cuts for the Wealthy*

Immediate Financial Benefits: One of the most direct benefits for Privileged White Americans in an authoritarian regime could be significant tax cuts. These cuts often target high-income earners and large estates, potentially resulting in increased disposable income for the wealthy.

Investment and Consumption: With more disposable income, there is an opportunity for increased investment in markets and luxury consumption, which can further stimulate sectors of the economy directly tied to the spending habits of the wealthy. This can create a positive feedback loop that initially boosts their financial portfolios and enhances their lifestyle.

## *Deregulation of Industries*

Business Growth and Expansion: Deregulation, a common hallmark of government shifts towards more centralized power, can lead to rapid business growth. Industries such as finance, energy, and manufacturing might see reduced compliance costs and fewer barriers to expansion, benefiting businesses typically owned by or catering to Privileged White Americans.

Innovation and Efficiency: Reduced regulatory burdens can also lead to increased innovation within these sectors. Companies might find new ways to maximize profits and efficiency without the constraints of stringent regulations. However, this reduction in oversight can also lead to negative environmental and social impacts, which are often overlooked in the short-term profitability calculus.

## *Reduced Corporate Oversight*

Enhanced Autonomy in Business Operations: With weaker oversight, corporations can operate with greater autonomy. This can allow for faster decision-making and reduced costs related to compliance with labor laws, environmental standards, and consumer protection regulations.

Profit Maximization: In the absence of strict oversight, businesses can often increase profits by cutting corners in areas like employee welfare, environmental protection, and product safety. While this can lead to greater profitability, it also raises ethical concerns and potential long-term societal costs.

## *Potential Risks and Limitations*

Sustainability of Economic Gains: While the immediate financial benefits can be substantial, the sustainability of these gains is questionable. Over-reliance on deregulation and tax cuts can lead to economic imbalances, asset bubbles, and increased inequality, which may eventually destabilize the economy.

Public Perception and Social Cohesion: The overt favoritism towards the wealthy can lead to increased social tensions and erode public trust in government institutions. This can manifest in social unrest, which might disrupt economic activities and negate some of the short-term gains.

## *Broader Economic Implications*

Impact on the General Economy: The broader economic implications of policies that favor the wealthy can be complex. While certain sectors may experience growth, the overall health of the economy can suffer due to increased inequality and reduced consumer spending power among the middle and lower classes.

International Repercussions: Internationally, such policies might lead to criticisms and sanctions from other nations, particularly those with stringent regulations on environmental standards and corporate governance. This could impact international markets and global standing, affecting businesses that operate across borders.

In Essence, The economic gains for Privileged White Americans under a move towards authoritarianism may appear attractive in the short term. Tax reductions, deregulation, and lax corporate oversight can lead to increased wealth and business opportunities for this demographic. However, these benefits must be weighed against the potential for long-term economic instability, ethical dilemmas, and the undermining of democratic norms. A comprehensive analysis reveals that while immediate financial benefits may accrue, the ultimate costs to society could be substantial, challenging the sustainability and morality of such gains.

# Political Influence: Concentration of Power and Its Implications for Privileged White Americans

In a political environment where power becomes increasingly concentrated, individuals and groups with existing influence, particularly Privileged White Americans, may find their ability to shape policy and government decisions significantly enhanced. This concentration of political power can lead to a system where connections, wealth, and status translate more directly into political clout. This section examines how these dynamics might manifest and the potential consequences for both the influencers and the broader society.

### *Access to Political Leaders*

Direct Access and Influence: As democratic checks and balances erode under authoritarian tendencies, those with existing social and economic power, including many Privileged White Americans, might find it easier to gain direct access to political leaders. This access can come through formal avenues, such as lobbying, or more informal ones, like social connections and private meetings.

Influence on Policy Making: With closer ties to political leaders, privileged groups can exert a disproportionate influence on policy formulation. This can include tailoring legislation to favor their business interests, securing favorable regulatory changes, or influencing tax policies to benefit the wealthy.

## *Shaping Legislative Agendas*

Setting Priorities: Influential groups might play a significant role in setting legislative agendas that align with their interests. This can lead to a focus on issues that are particularly beneficial to them, such as deregulation, tax relief for high earners, and protections for established industries.

Marginalization of Broader Interests: As a result, the broader public interest may be sidelined in favor of the priorities of the elite. Issues such as income inequality, social welfare, environmental protection, and workers' rights might receive less attention or be actively undermined.

## *Regulatory Capture*

Control Over Regulatory Bodies: There is a risk of regulatory capture, where key industry stakeholders gain control over the agencies meant to regulate them. This can lead to weaker enforcement of laws that are supposed to protect the public and the environment but may conflict with business interests.

Long-Term Impacts: Over time, regulatory capture can lead to systemic inefficiencies and corruption, eroding the quality of governance and public trust in institutions. This can have widespread economic consequences, including reduced competition and innovation.

## *Cronyism and Patronage*

Expansion of Crony Networks: In a system where political power is concentrated, the practice of cronyism can flourish. Political leaders may reward loyal supporters with government positions, contracts, or business advantages, further entrenching the power of privileged groups.

Perpetuation of Inequality: Such practices can perpetuate social and economic inequality, as they limit opportunities for those outside the established networks of power and influence. This can stifle social mobility and widen the gap between the elite and the rest of the population.

## *Potential Backlash*

Social and Political Repercussions: While Privileged White Americans may find increased political influence beneficial in the short term, there is a potential for significant backlash. Discontent can grow among the broader population as they perceive the political system to be rigged in favor of a select few.

Calls for Reform: This discontent may eventually fuel movements calling for political reform and greater transparency. If such movements gain enough momentum, they can lead to significant shifts in political power and policy priorities, potentially reversing gains made by privileged groups.

## *Strategies for Mitigating Negative Impacts*

Promoting Transparency and Accountability: it is vital to promote greater transparency and accountability in government dealings. To mitigate the negative impacts of concentrated political influence, This includes stronger regulations on lobbying, more open legislative processes, and enhanced scrutiny of policy decisions.

Fostering Civic Engagement: Encouraging broader civic engagement can help balance the influence of privileged groups. Supporting grassroots movements, public forums, and community organizing can empower a wider spectrum of the population to participate in the political process.

In Essence While the concentration of political power might initially benefit Privileged White Americans, allowing them to shape policies and decisions in their favor, it poses significant risks to democratic governance and social equality. The long-term sustainability of such a system is questionable, as it can lead to social unrest and demands for substantial political reform. Therefore, all stakeholders must consider the broader implications of such power dynamics and work towards a more balanced and fair political system.

# Chapter 2: Loss of Political Voice

# Restricted Voting Rights: Implications of Eroding Democratic Institutions

As democratic institutions face erosion under authoritarian-leaning governance, one of the most alarming consequences is the restriction of voting rights. These restrictions can fundamentally alter the democratic process, limiting the ability of citizens, including Privileged White Americans, to influence political decisions effectively. This section explores how the curtailment of voting rights could manifest, its implications, and the broader impact on democratic engagement.

## *Mechanisms of Voting Restrictions*

Stricter Voter ID Laws: One common method to restrict voting is the implementation of stringent voter ID laws. These laws often disproportionately affect minority and lower-income voters. Still, the overall reduction in voter turnout can shift political dynamics substantially, impacting all demographics.

Reduction of Voting Access: This can include reducing the number of polling places, limiting early voting and mail-in voting options, and purging voter rolls. While these measures may be presented as efforts to secure the electoral process, they can significantly impede the ability of citizens to vote.

## *Impact on Voter Turnout*

Disenfranchisement: By making it harder to vote, these restrictions can disenfranchise large segments of the population. Reduced participation weakens the representative nature of elections as the electorate becomes less reflective of the population's diversity.

Erosion of Public Trust: As voting becomes more difficult and perceptions of electoral fairness decline, public trust in the electoral process and the legitimacy of elected officials can diminish. This cynicism can lead to lower engagement in future elections, further eroding democratic norms.

## *Consequences for Political Influence*

Shifts in Political Power: With voting restrictions in place, the composition of the electorate can shift, often favoring groups less affected by the restrictions, such as economically privileged individuals. However, as the overall voter base narrows, the political landscape can become more volatile, with power concentrated in fewer hands.

Limitation of Policy Impact: For Privileged White Americans, restricted voting rights can mean that while they may still hold significant economic and social influence, their ability to shape policy through the ballot box can diminish if broader public participation wanes and political stability is threatened.

## Long-Term Democratic Implications

Weakening of Democratic Institutions: Continuous restrictions on voting rights can lead to a significant weakening of democratic institutions. Over time, if elections are perceived as unfair or unrepresentative, the fundamental democratic principle of government by the people is undermined.

Potential for Authoritarian Consolidation: In the absence of robust voter turnout and fair participation, the path is clearer for authoritarian figures to consolidate power, often under the guise of rectifying the very irregularities their policies have exacerbated.

## Strategies for Mitigation and Advocacy

Legal Challenges and Advocacy: Legal avenues remain a crucial method for challenging restrictive voting laws. Advocacy groups can work to overturn or amend laws that curtail voting rights through litigation and public campaigns.

Promotion of Voting Rights Legislation: Supporting legislation that protects and expands voting rights is essential. This includes advocating for laws that enhance voter registration, extend voting times, and protect against disenfranchisement.

## Civic Engagement and Education

Voter Education Campaigns: comprehensive voter education campaigns are necessary To counteract the effects of restricted voting rights. These campaigns can inform voters about their rights, the importance of their vote, and how to navigate the voting process despite new restrictions.

Community Mobilization: Mobilizing community efforts to support voters, such as organizing rides to polling places or providing assistance with voter registration, can help mitigate the impact of restrictive voting measures.

In Essence The restriction of voting rights as a consequence of democratic erosion poses significant challenges not just to marginalized groups but to all demographics, including Privileged White Americans. While they may initially experience less direct impact, the overall weakening of democratic processes and the resultant shifts in political power can have profound long-term consequences. Active resistance to these trends through legal, legislative, and civic channels is crucial to preserving the integrity and inclusiveness of the democratic system.

# Suppression of Dissent: The Impact on Democratic Expression

The suppression of dissent is a hallmark of authoritarian regimes and a significant threat to democratic freedoms. In environments where the ruling party seeks to consolidate power, measures to stifle dissenting voices can become increasingly severe, impacting not only traditional opposition groups but also members of the majority who may disagree with certain policies or actions. This section examines how the suppression of dissent might manifest, the consequences for democratic dialogue, and the broader implications for society.

### *Mechanisms of Suppressing Dissent*

Legislative Tools: Governments may enact laws that ostensibly aim to protect national security or public order but are actually designed to curtail free speech and peaceful assembly. These laws can impose severe penalties for participating in protests, speaking against the government, or even expressing dissent on social media platforms.

Judicial Actions: Courts can be used as tools to enforce suppression, where dissenters face harsh sentences for minor infractions. This judicial harshness serves as a deterrent to others who might consider speaking out against the government.

## Impact on Public Protests

Criminalization of Protest: One of the most visible forms of dissent suppression is the criminalization of public protests. Authorities may label peaceful demonstrations as riots or unlawful assemblies, leading to mass arrests and criminal charges for participants.

Use of Force: Law enforcement agencies may be given broad discretion to use force in managing protests, leading to escalated confrontations. The use of tear gas, water cannons, and even live ammunition can be justified under the guise of maintaining public order.

## Censorship and Media Control

Media Restrictions: The government might impose stringent controls on media outlets, censoring news that is critical of the ruling party or that discusses the dissent. This includes blocking access to websites, penalizing journalists, and shuttering media institutions under various pretexts.

Surveillance and Monitoring: Increased surveillance of citizens, particularly those known to dissent, is another tactic. Monitoring of internet activity, phone calls, and even personal interactions can suppress dissent by creating a climate of fear and paranoia.

## Consequences for Political Discourse

Chilling Effect on Free Speech: The fear of reprisal can lead to a chilling effect, where individuals and groups choose to self-censor rather than risk the consequences of expressing dissent. This stifles healthy political discourse and deprives society of diverse opinions and debates.

Erosion of Democratic Norms: Over time, the systematic suppression of dissent erodes foundational democratic norms such as freedom of expression, the right to assemble, and the right to a fair trial. This degradation can transform the democratic landscape into one where authoritarian practices become normalized.

## Implications for Social Cohesion

Polarization and Alienation: The suppression of dissent can lead to increased social polarization. As people are unable to express their grievances freely, frustration and anger may build, leading to further alienation from the political system.

Potential for Radicalization: In extreme cases, the suppression of peaceful dissent may push individuals towards more radical means of expression. This can lead to a cycle of violence and repression that is detrimental to societal stability.

## Strategies for Resistance and Advocacy

Legal and International Advocacy: Legal challenges to suppressive laws and international advocacy can play crucial roles in resisting the suppression of dissent. Organizations and individuals can seek support from international human rights bodies and foreign governments to pressure the regime to alter its approach.

Coalition Building: Building broad-based coalitions that include a variety of social groups can strengthen the resistance against suppression. These coalitions can provide mutual support, share resources, and amplify the voices of dissent through united fronts.

In Essence The suppression of dissent is a critical issue that poses a direct threat to the health and sustainability of democratic societies. Understanding and addressing the mechanisms through which dissent is suppressed is vital for maintaining democratic norms and ensuring that all voices can be heard. Advocacy, legal action, and international cooperation are essential tools in combating these authoritarian tendencies and preserving the fundamental rights that underpin democratic governance.

# Chapter 3: Economic Impacts

# Maintenance of Status Quo: Reinforcement of Social Status and Cultural Norms

In the context of a shift toward authoritarianism, Privileged White Americans might find that such a regime supports and reinforces their existing social status and cultural norms. This perceived alignment can initially appear beneficial, as it seemingly protects established privileges and promotes traditional values. This section delves into how an authoritarian regime might favor certain societal values and traditions, the implications for privileged groups, and the broader impact on societal dynamics.

## *Reinforcement of Traditional Values*

Promotion of Conservative Cultural Norms: Authoritarian regimes often promote conservative cultural norms and values that resonate with traditionalist segments of society, including many Privileged White Americans. This can include policies that reinforce traditional family structures, religious values, and nationalistic sentiments.

Legislation Reflecting Conservative Ideals: Laws may be enacted that reflect these conservative values, such as restrictions on progressive social movements, educational curricula that favor a traditionalist viewpoint, and public endorsements of specific cultural identities and histories.

## *Social Status Preservation*

Protection of Economic Interests: Authoritarian regimes might implement economic policies that protect the wealth and property of the upper classes, ensuring that the economic disparities that underpin social hierarchies are maintained or even exacerbated.

Exclusivity in Policy Making: By keeping decision-making circles exclusive and aligned with their interests, Privileged White Americans might feel their social status is not only protected but endorsed by the state's power structures.

## *Social and Racial Segregation*

Enforcement of Segregation Policies: In efforts to maintain the status quo, authoritarian regimes may subtly or overtly support social and racial segregation. This could manifest in housing policies, schooling, and public services that keep different social and racial groups separate and unequal.

Institutionalization of Inequalities: Long-standing inequalities may be institutionalized under authoritarian rule, with laws and policies that make it challenging to address disparities in wealth, access to resources, and representation in governance.

## Impact on Social Cohesion

Deepening Social Divides: While reinforcing traditional values and norms might appeal to some, such policies can alienate and marginalize other groups within society, deepening social divides. This can lead to increased tensions and conflict between different demographic groups.

Suppression of Alternative Views: The authoritarian suppression of dissenting or alternative views can prevent meaningful dialogue and change, stifling social progress and the evolution of more inclusive cultural norms.

## Long-Term Consequences

Cultural Stagnation: While maintaining the status quo might seem beneficial in the short term, it can lead to cultural stagnation in the long run. Societies that do not adapt to changing times and demographics are at risk of losing their dynamism and capacity to innovate.

Resistance and Backlash: Over time, the broader population's dissatisfaction with the maintenance of outdated or unfair status quo can lead to significant resistance. This could manifest in social movements, protests, and, in some cases, violent conflicts.

## Strategies for Broader Engagement

Promotion of Inclusive Policies: To mitigate these risks, it is important for all sectors of society, including privileged groups, to advocate for more inclusive and forward-looking policies that consider the well-being of the entire population.

Encouraging Dialogue and Reconciliation: Programs that foster dialogue and reconciliation between different social and cultural groups can help bridge divides and create a more cohesive society.

In Essence While the maintenance of the status quo under an authoritarian regime might initially seem favorable to Privileged White Americans, the long-term implications can be detrimental to social cohesion and the democratic fabric of society. The reinforcement of traditional values and norms at the expense of suppressing diversity and stifling progress can lead to cultural stagnation and social unrest. For a healthy, dynamic society, it is crucial to embrace inclusivity and adaptability, ensuring that all citizens feel valued and have the opportunity to contribute to societal development.

# Income Inequality: The Widening Gap Between Rich and Poor

The shift toward policies that disproportionately favor the wealthy, often a characteristic of authoritarian regimes, can significantly exacerbate income inequality. While Privileged White Americans might initially benefit from such policies, the average Privileged White Americans, especially those not in the upper economic echelons, could face a different reality. This section explores how the economic policies under an authoritarian regime could widen the gap between the rich and the poor, leading to stagnant wages and diminished economic opportunities for the majority of the population.

## *Economic Policies Favoring the Wealthy*

Tax Cuts and Benefits for the Rich: Authoritarian regimes may implement significant tax cuts for the wealthy and for large corporations under the guise of stimulating economic growth. While these cuts can increase the disposable income for the rich, they often lead to a decrease in public revenues, which can affect funding for social services and welfare programs that benefit the broader population.

Deregulation Favoring Established Businesses: Deregulation efforts may be aimed primarily at benefiting industries dominated by the wealthy, reducing costs and increasing profits for those at the top while potentially compromising employee welfare, consumer protection, and environmental standards.

## Impact on Wages and Employment

Stagnant or Declining Wages: With a focus on boosting corporate profits, wages for average workers, including many Privileged White Americans not in the upper classes, might stagnate or even decline. This is often exacerbated by weakened labor unions and reduced bargaining power, which are typical in authoritarian settings.

Job Insecurity and Quality: The quality of jobs may also deteriorate, with fewer benefits and job security. Economic policies might encourage the growth of part-time and contract work over full-time, stable employment, leading to greater economic vulnerability for the average worker.

## Reduced Economic Opportunities

Impact on Small Businesses and Startups: Favoritism toward large corporations can stifle competition, making it difficult for small businesses and startups to thrive. This limits economic opportunities for average individuals who do not have the capital to compete on a larger scale.

Limited Social Mobility: Economic policies that favor the wealthy can lead to reduced social mobility. With escalating costs for education and healthcare and diminishing public services, the average individual finds it increasingly challenging to improve their economic status.

## Social Consequences of Growing Inequality

Increased Social Stratification: As the economic divide widens, so too does social stratification. This can lead to segregated communities and a lack of interaction between different social classes, further entrenching disparities.

Erosion of Social Cohesion: High levels of income inequality can erode social cohesion and lead to increased tension and unrest. Disparities in wealth and opportunity can fuel resentment and lead to social instability.

## Long-Term Implications for Economic Health

Economic Instability: While the wealthy may experience short-term gains, the broader economy could suffer from long-term instability. A consumer base with diminished purchasing power cannot sustain high levels of economic growth.

Inefficiencies and Corruption: Policies that favor the wealthy often lead to inefficiencies in the economy and can increase corruption as elites manipulate the system to maintain their economic status.

## Policy Recommendations to Address Income Inequality

Progressive Taxation: Implementing a progressive tax system can ensure that the wealthy contribute a fair share to the economy, facilitating redistribution and funding for essential public services.

Strengthening Worker Protections and Wages: Laws that protect workers' rights promote fair wages, and support unionization can help balance the power between employers and employees, leading to better wages and job security.

Investment in Public Services: Investing in education, healthcare, and infrastructure can promote greater social mobility and economic opportunities for all, reducing the gap between the rich and the poor.

In Essence, While policies favoring the wealthy might enrich a small segment of society, they typically do so at the expense of the broader population, including average Privileged White Americans. It is essential to implement policies that promote fair wages, protect workers, and ensure economic opportunities for all citizens To foster a more equitable society. Addressing income inequality is not only a matter of economic justice. Still, it is crucial for maintaining social stability and ensuring sustainable economic growth.

# Deregulation: Assessing the Broad Impacts on Society and the Environment

Deregulation is often championed as a means to reduce bureaucratic red tape and bolster business efficiency and profitability. However, the broader impacts of deregulation can be profound and multifaceted, affecting not just the economic sphere but also worker protection, environmental health, and public safety. This section explores the potential consequences of deregulation, especially when implemented without careful consideration of its wider effects.

## *Economic Benefits and Costs*

Short-Term Economic Gains: Initially, deregulation can lead to significant economic benefits for certain sectors, particularly industries like manufacturing, energy, and finance, which may experience growth due to lower compliance costs and fewer operational restrictions.

Long-Term Economic Risks: Over time, the absence of regulatory oversight can lead to market failures, monopolistic practices, and financial crises. Deregulation in financial markets, for example, has historically led to bubbles and crashes due to insufficient oversight of risky practices.

## *Impact on Worker Protections*

Weakening of Safety Standards: Deregulation often involves cutting back on labor protections to reduce costs for businesses. This can lead to weaker safety standards in workplaces, increased risk of accidents, and less accountability from employers.

Erosion of Labor Rights: Reduced regulations can also undermine workers' rights, including the right to organize, fair wages, and adequate working conditions. This erosion can lead to more precarious employment terms, lower job security, and increased inequality within the workforce.

## *Environmental Consequences*

Environmental Degradation: One of the most significant impacts of deregulation is on the environment. Loosening environmental controls can lead to increased pollution, habitat destruction, and unsustainable exploitation of natural resources.

Climate Change Acceleration: Specific deregulatory measures, such as relaxing emissions standards for industries and vehicles, can contribute to an increase in greenhouse gas emissions, thereby accelerating climate change and its associated impacts on weather patterns, sea levels, and biodiversity.

## Public Health Implications

Increased Health Risks: Deregulation can also compromise public health standards, for instance, by allowing more pollutants in the air and water or by reducing food safety standards. This can lead to higher incidences of respiratory and cardiovascular diseases and foodborne illnesses among the population.

The strain on Healthcare Systems: As public health deteriorates due to poorer environmental and workplace standards, there can be a corresponding increase in healthcare costs and greater strain on public health services.

## Quality of Life

Degradation of Quality of Life: The cumulative impact of reduced worker protections, environmental degradation, and public health risks can significantly degrade the quality of life for many individuals. This is particularly true for communities in proximity to deregulated industries or those who rely on natural resources for their livelihoods.

Disproportionate Impact on Vulnerable Populations: Often, the negative effects of deregulation disproportionately impact the most vulnerable segments of society: low-income communities, minorities, and those without the means to mitigate exposure to environmental or occupational hazards.

## Policy Recommendations

Balanced Regulatory Approaches: Policymakers should aim for a balanced approach to regulation, one that protects public and environmental health without imposing unnecessary burdens on businesses. This can involve regular reviews of regulatory frameworks to adapt to new technologies and scientific findings.

Stakeholder Engagement: Including a wide range of stakeholders in the regulatory process can ensure that diverse perspectives are considered, particularly those of vulnerable communities and workers who are most impacted by deregulation.

In Essence, While deregulation may provide certain economic benefits, its broader implications reveal significant risks and costs to society. Effective regulation is not about stifling business but protecting broader societal interests, including worker safety, public health, and environmental sustainability. Recognizing and mitigating the potential negative impacts of deregulation is crucial for ensuring that the economy serves the well-being of all citizens, not just the interests of a few.

# Control Over Education and Media: Reinforcing Dominant Worldviews

In an environment where authoritarian tendencies begin to take root, control over key cultural and informational institutions like education and media becomes a strategic priority. For Privileged White Americans, or indeed any dominant group within a society shifting toward authoritarianism, exerting influence over these sectors can serve to maintain and strengthen their social position. This control not only solidifies their worldview within the public sphere but also limits exposure to dissenting perspectives, creating a more homogeneous cultural and political landscape.

## *Control Over Education*

Curriculum Design and Content: By influencing educational curricula, privileged groups can ensure that the educational system reflects and reinforces their values and beliefs. This might include the promotion of certain historical narratives, the omission of controversial or minority perspectives, and the emphasis on traditional roles and ideologies.

Institutional Influence: Influence can also extend to the governance of educational institutions. Appointments of school boards, university trustees, and other key positions can be skewed towards individuals who support or belong to the privileged group, further entrenching their control over educational policies and practices.

## Dominance in Media

Media Ownership and Censorship: Owning or influencing media outlets is a powerful tool for controlling public discourse. This control can manifest through the promotion of specific political and cultural messages that align with the group's interests while censoring or underreporting opposing views.

Shaping Public Opinion: Media has the power to shape public opinion and cultural norms. By controlling the media narrative, privileged groups can craft and disseminate a cohesive and persuasive worldview that minimizes the visibility and impact of alternative viewpoints.

## Limiting Exposure to Diverse Perspectives

Echo Chambers: Control over education and media contributes to the creation of echo chambers where individuals are primarily exposed to ideas and opinions that reinforce their own. This lack of exposure to diverse perspectives can reduce critical thinking and increase polarization within society.

Suppressing Dissent: By controlling the flow of information and the content of education, dissenting opinions can be effectively marginalized or presented as fringe, illegitimate, or dangerous. This suppression plays a critical role in maintaining the status quo and reducing challenges to the dominant group's authority and perspective.

## Cultural Homogenization

Standardization of Culture: Through media and education, there is a potential for cultural homogenization, where diverse identities and stories are subsumed under a dominant narrative that celebrates certain values, traditions, and histories at the expense of others.

Loss of Cultural Diversity: As alternative voices and histories are sidelined, the rich diversity of cultural expressions and narratives can be lost, leading to a less vibrant and dynamic society.

## *Broader Societal Implications*

Weakening of Democratic Discourse: A healthy democracy relies on a well-informed citizenry and a vibrant exchange of ideas. Control over education and media can weaken democratic discourse by limiting the range of debate and restricting informed decision-making.

The entrenchment of Power: As these control mechanisms solidify, they create structural barriers to change, making it difficult for future generations to challenge or alter the established order. This entrenchment can perpetuate inequalities and hinder social progress.

## *Strategies for Mitigation*

Regulatory Safeguards: Implementing robust regulatory frameworks that ensure diversity and fairness in media ownership and educational content can help counteract tendencies toward control and censorship.

Support for Alternative Media and Educational Initiatives: Encouraging and supporting independent media outlets and alternative educational initiatives can ensure that diverse voices and perspectives are heard, promoting a more inclusive public discourse.

In Essence The control over education and media by privileged groups within an authoritarian-leaning society can significantly impact the cultural and political landscape. While it may reinforce the dominant group's worldview and suppress dissent, the long-term consequences for democratic health and cultural diversity are profound. Addressing these issues requires a concerted effort to promote diversity, transparency, and inclusivity in these critical sectors, ensuring a balanced and democratic exchange of ideas essential for a healthy society.

# Chapter 4: Social and Cultural Shifts

# Increased Polarization: The Impact of Identity Politics on Social Cohesion

The strategic deployment of identity politics as a tool to consolidate power can have profound and lasting effects on societal cohesion in environments where political strategies intensively focus on accentuating divisions, whether based on race, ethnicity, religion, or other social identifiers, communities can become increasingly fragmented. This fragmentation often leads to increased polarization, which can escalate into social unrest and contribute to a more contentious and insecure daily life for all citizens.

## *Mechanisms of Polarization through Identity Politics*

Exploitation of Social Divides: Politicians and power groups may exploit existing social divides as a means to rally support, creating an "us vs. them" narrative. This can be seen in political rhetoric that categorizes groups as either allies or threats, often oversimplifying complex social issues into binary choices.

Legislative and Policy Initiatives: Policies may be introduced that overtly favor one group over another or penalize certain identities, reinforcing divisions and perpetuating grievances among marginalized or opposing groups.

## *Consequences for Community Relations*

Erosion of Trust: As communities are pitted against each other, trust between different social groups can significantly erode. The lack of trust makes cooperative and harmonious living difficult as individuals grow more suspicious and protective against perceived threats from 'out-groups.'

Increased Social Friction: Daily interactions may become more fraught with tension as identity-based politics heighten awareness of differences and grievances. This can manifest in social avoidance, verbal conflicts, or even violent confrontations in communities.

## *Impact on Public Safety and Security*

Social Unrest: Heightened polarization may lead to increased social unrest, including protests, riots, and clashes between different community groups. These events can disrupt daily life, lead to the destruction of property, and, in severe cases, result in injuries or loss of life.

Strain on Law Enforcement: Frequent social unrest puts considerable strain on public safety and law enforcement agencies. Police may become overstretched and may also be perceived as taking sides, which can further exacerbate tensions and undermine the rule of law.

## Economic Implications

Impact on Local Economies: Polarization and social unrest can have detrimental effects on local economies. Businesses may suffer from regular disruptions, decreased customer traffic, and higher costs for security and insurance. This economic downturn can exacerbate the living conditions of all residents, particularly those in already vulnerable positions.

Discouragement of Investment: Areas experiencing high levels of social unrest and polarization might find it difficult to attract or retain investment. Potential investors often seek stable and secure environments, and visible social divisions can be a significant deterrent.

## Mitigating the Effects of Polarization

Promoting Inclusive Dialogue: Efforts to foster dialogue and understanding between different community groups can help mitigate polarization. Initiatives like community forums, intergroup dialogues, and collaborative community projects can bridge divides and foster a sense of common purpose.

Education and Awareness Campaigns: Educational campaigns that promote diversity, inclusivity, and the value of multiculturalism can counteract the divisive effects of identity politics. Schools and community centers can play critical roles in these educational efforts.

## Policy Interventions

Fair Representation in Policy Making: Ensuring that all community groups have fair representation in the policy-making process can help alleviate feelings of marginalization and injustice. Policies should be crafted with the input and consideration of diverse community perspectives to ensure they meet the needs of all, not just the majority or the most powerful.

Legal Protections Against Discrimination: Strong legal frameworks that protect against discrimination and promote equal rights for all citizens are crucial in countering divisive identity politics. These laws must be robustly enforced to be effective.

In Essence The use of identity politics to consolidate power is a dangerous strategy that can lead to deepened divisions within society, increasing polarization and social unrest. These dynamics make daily life more contentious and insecure, affecting community cohesion and economic stability. To counteract these trends, a concerted effort from all sectors of society, including government, community leaders, and citizens, is essential to promote inclusivity, dialogue, and mutual respect.

# Education and Information Control: Impact on Perspective and Cultural Interaction

Strategic control over education and media is a significant method employed by authoritarian regimes to shape societal views and limit the exposure of the population to diverse perspectives. For Privileged White Americans, these efforts could drastically narrow their worldview, altering their perception of various issues and their interactions with different cultures. This section delves into how controlling education and information can shape public opinion and behavior, reinforcing certain ideologies while suppressing alternative viewpoints.

### *Control Over Education*

Curriculum Manipulation: Authoritarian control often involves the manipulation of educational curricula to promote specific ideologies. This could include the glorification of certain historical narratives, the omission of critical historical events, and the marginalization of contributions from diverse cultures. Such an education system teaches a skewed version of history and social studies, impacting students' understanding of their country and the world.

Suppression of Academic Freedom: In higher education, the suppression of academic freedom can stifle scholarly debate and research, particularly in fields like social sciences, humanities, and political science. When educators are restricted to teaching only government-approved materials, students' exposure to a broad range of theories and perspectives is significantly limited.

## *Media Control and Censorship*

Information Filtering: Control over media, whether through censorship, ownership of media outlets, or legal pressures, allows a government to filter and dictate the information that reaches the public. This control can ensure that only government-sanctioned messages are disseminated, effectively shaping public perception to align with authoritarian views.

Propaganda and Misinformation: The use of media to spread propaganda further entrenches controlled views. By consistently presenting information that supports certain ideologies while denigrating or ignoring alternative viewpoints, the media under authoritarian regimes can deeply influence how people perceive social, political, and cultural issues.

## *Impact on Cultural Perception and Interaction*

Narrow Worldview: A lack of exposure to diverse cultures and perspectives can lead to a narrow, often ethnocentric worldview among Privileged White Americans. This limited perspective can affect their ability to empathize with or understand the challenges faced by people from different backgrounds.

Biased Perceptions: With a media and education system that predominantly reflects and reinforces the dominant group's viewpoints, Privileged White Americans may develop biased perceptions towards other cultures, potentially harboring stereotypes or misconceptions that are seldom challenged by authoritative or alternative sources.

## *Social Consequences*

Reduced Social Cohesion: The controlled and narrow dissemination of information can exacerbate social divides, reducing cohesion and understanding between different cultural and social groups within the country.

Xenophobia and Nationalism: In some cases, the promotion of a singular national identity and the suppression of multicultural elements can foster xenophobic attitudes and heightened nationalism. This can manifest in hostile attitudes and policies towards immigrants and minorities.

## *Mitigating Measures*

Promotion of Media Literacy: Educating citizens about media literacy to critically analyze and question the information they receive can help counteract the effects of controlled media. This includes understanding the sources of information and recognizing biases and propaganda.

Support for Independent Media and Educational Institutions: Encouraging and supporting independent media outlets and educational institutions that promote diverse viewpoints can provide alternative sources of information, helping to broaden perspectives and foster a more informed citizenry.

Cultural Exchange Programs: Implementing and supporting cultural exchange programs can expose individuals to diverse cultures and perspectives, promoting greater understanding and appreciation of global diversity.

In Essence Efforts to control education and media can profoundly impact how Privileged White Americans perceive and interact with the world, often leading to a more insular and skewed understanding of diverse cultures and global issues. It is crucial to encourage open access to a variety of perspectives and promote the values of diversity and critical thinking in all aspects of education and media consumption. To foster a more inclusive and accurate worldview,

# Growing Inequality: Social Unrest and Its Impact on Privileged White Americans

The escalation of income and social inequality is a breeding ground for social unrest, particularly when large segments of the population feel marginalized and oppressed by an unfair economic and social system. For Privileged White Americans, who might be perceived as beneficiaries or perpetuators of these inequalities, the backlash could manifest in various disruptive ways. This section explores how increased inequality can lead to social unrest, the potential forms of backlash against privileged groups, and the broader implications for societal stability.

## *Drivers of Inequality*

Economic Disparities: Economic policies that favor the wealthy can exacerbate income disparities, with the rich getting richer. At the same time, wages and living standards stagnate or decline for the majority. This disparity can breed resentment and a sense of injustice among those who see no improvement in their economic situation.

Limited Social Mobility: When people feel that structural barriers block their opportunities to improve their economic status, the frustration can lead to disillusionment with the system. This includes barriers in education, employment, and access to healthcare, which are often felt more acutely by minority communities.

## *Manifestations of Social Unrest*

Public Protests: One of the most visible signs of social unrest due to growing inequality is an increase in public protests. These demonstrations can vary in scale and intensity, from peaceful marches to significant disruptions involving thousands of participants expressing their grievances.

Strikes and Work Stoppages: Labor strikes and work stoppages can also occur more frequently as workers demand better wages, benefits, and working conditions. These actions not only highlight the economic aspects of inequality but can disrupt industries and economies, impacting society at large, including privileged groups.

## Backlash Against Privileged Groups

Direct Confrontations: Privileged White Americans might face confrontations during protests and public demonstrations, where they are seen as symbols of the inequitable status quo. This can lead to uncomfortable or hostile encounters, particularly in communities with stark economic divides.

Reputational Risks: There is also a reputational risk as groups that are perceived to maintain or benefit from inequality might be publicly criticized or boycotted. This could affect businesses owned by privileged individuals, impacting their social standing and economic interests.

## Heightened Tensions and Violence

Escalation to Violence: In some cases, prolonged or extreme inequality can lead to outbreaks of violence. This might include rioting or clashes between different social groups and law enforcement. Such violence not only disrupts daily life but can lead to lasting damage to properties, neighborhoods, and community relations.

Security Concerns: The fear of violence can lead to increased security measures by individuals and communities, often resulting in fortified homes and gated communities. This can deepen social divisions, creating physical and symbolic barriers between different economic classes.

## Mitigating Social Unrest

Policy Reforms: Addressing the root causes of inequality through comprehensive policy reforms is crucial. This includes reforming tax systems, increasing the minimum wage, and investing in social services that provide a safety net for the most vulnerable populations.

Community Engagement and Dialogue: Promoting dialogue between disparate social groups can help mitigate tensions. Initiatives that foster understanding and collaboration across economic divides can reduce misconceptions and build a more cohesive community.

### *Building Resilient Communities*

Inclusive Development: Encouraging development projects that benefit all community members can help alleviate feelings of exclusion and marginalization. This includes equitable urban planning, affordable housing, and accessible public services.

Education and Awareness Programs: Educating the public about the impacts of inequality and the benefits of a more equitable society can change perceptions and encourage more people to support inclusive policies.

In Essence As inequality grows, the potential for social unrest increases, potentially disrupting the lives of all citizens, including those who are privileged. Addressing these disparities through thoughtful, inclusive policies and fostering a culture of dialogue and cooperation is essential for maintaining societal stability and ensuring that all individuals can live in a fair and just society.

## Isolation from the Broader Population: Social Dynamics and Divisions

As the socio-political landscape evolves under authoritarian tendencies, Privileged White Americans who are perceived as supporting or benefiting from such a regime might find themselves increasingly isolated from the broader population. This isolation can manifest as social resentment, strained relationships, and even divisions within communities that traditionally enjoyed cohesion and privilege. This section explores how these dynamics might unfold, the impacts on social cohesion, and the potential for fracturing within privileged circles themselves.

### *Perceptions of Complicity*

Association with Authoritarian Policies: If Privileged White Americans are seen as key beneficiaries or active supporters of authoritarian policies, they may be perceived as complicit in any negative outcomes of these policies. This association can lead to resentment and mistrust from other demographic groups who feel adversely affected by the regime's actions.

Blame for Social and Economic Issues: In times of hardship or discontent, marginalized groups or those suffering under new policies might blame privileged circles for perpetuating their struggles, seeing them as part of the systemic problem rather than allies in the search for solutions.

## Social Resentment and Isolation

Withdrawal from Community Engagement: As tensions rise, privileged groups might withdraw from broader community engagement to avoid confrontation or criticism. This withdrawal can lead to increased social isolation, reinforcing the divide between them and other community members.

Targeted Social Backlash: Privileged individuals might face targeted backlash in social settings, community forums, or public discourse. This could include verbal criticisms, social ostracism, or organized protests against businesses and institutions associated with them.

## Strained Relationships within Communities

Erosion of Community Trust: The perceived alignment of Privileged White Americans with an authoritarian regime can erode trust within the community. Trust is a fundamental aspect of community cohesion, and its loss can lead to a breakdown in cooperative relationships and community-based initiatives.

Heightened Community Divisions: Communities might experience heightened divisions as individuals and groups take sides based on their support or opposition to the regime. These divisions can disrupt local governance, community projects, and even day-to-day interactions, leading to a fragmented society.

## Divisions within Privileged Circles

Differing Levels of Support: Not all Privileged White Americans may support the authoritarian shift. This variance in political and moral views can lead to internal conflicts, dividing families, friends, and social networks.

Pressure to Conform: Within privileged circles, there might be social pressure to conform to the dominant political stance. Those who dissent or criticize the regime may face social repercussions, including exclusion from social events, business opportunities, and community leadership roles.

## *Mitigating Social Isolation and Building Bridges*

Promoting Open Dialogue: Encouraging open and respectful dialogue between different groups can help reduce misunderstandings and mitigate resentment. Facilitated discussions, community forums, and intergroup workshops can be effective in bridging divides.

Community Reconciliation Initiatives: Implementing reconciliation initiatives that focus on healing and understanding can help restore trust and rebuild community cohesion. These initiatives could involve collaborative community service projects, shared cultural events, and public acknowledgments of past grievances.

## *Awareness and Self-Reflection*

Education on Authoritarian Impacts: Educating privileged groups about the broader impacts of authoritarian policies on different segments of the population can foster greater empathy and understanding.

Self-Reflection and Responsibility: Encouraging self-reflection among Privileged White Americans about their role and impact within the community can lead to more conscientious participation in public life and a reevaluation of their political and social stances.

In Essence The potential social isolation of Privileged White Americans in an authoritarian-leaning context underscores the complex interplay of socio-political identities and community dynamics. By understanding these processes and actively working to address and bridge divides, communities can work towards a more inclusive and cohesive social framework, even in challenging political times.

# Chapter 5: Erosion of Civil Liberties

# Surveillance and Privacy: The Impact of Increased Government Monitoring

In an authoritarian regime, the expansion of government surveillance and the erosion of privacy rights are common phenomena. These measures are often justified on grounds of national security. Still, they can have profound implications for the personal freedoms of all citizens, including average Privileged White Americans. This shift towards more pervasive monitoring can lead to greater scrutiny of everyday activities and communications, affecting various aspects of daily life.

## *Expansion of Surveillance Measures*

Technological Monitoring: Advances in technology allow for more sophisticated surveillance methods. This could include mass data collection from smartphones, social media, and even through increasingly interconnected 'smart' home devices. Average citizens might find their digital footprints being constantly monitored and analyzed by government entities.

Physical Surveillance: Increased use of CCTV cameras in public spaces, facial recognition technology, and other forms of physical monitoring can make public outings less private. The feeling of being constantly watched can alter behaviors and limit the freedom to move and act freely in public spaces.

## *Reduction of Privacy Rights*

Legal Changes: An authoritarian regime might pass legislation that reduces legal protections for privacy. This could include laws that make it easier for government agencies to access personal data without a warrant or that require companies to provide government access to customer data.

Normalization of Surveillance: Over time, the public might become desensitized to these intrusions, gradually accepting them as a 'new normal.' This normalization can significantly alter societal expectations of privacy and personal space.

## *Impact on Daily Life*

Self-Censorship: With the knowledge that their communications and activities might be monitored, individuals might begin to self-censor their expressions both online and offline. This can stifle free speech and restrict open dialogue on potentially controversial topics.

Stress and Anxiety: The psychological impact of constant surveillance can lead to increased stress and anxiety. The fear of having one's private actions misinterpreted or used against them by authorities can create a pervasive sense of insecurity.

## *Implications for Social Interactions*

Distrust in Communications: Knowing that communications could be monitored might lead people to distrust electronic forms of communication, potentially impacting relationships and social interactions. Conversations may become more guarded, and individuals might avoid discussing sensitive topics even with close friends and family.

Impact on Social Cohesion: The overall impact on social cohesion can be negative, as surveillance fosters an environment of suspicion and fear. This can weaken community bonds and reduce the sense of solidarity among different groups within society.

## *Resistance and Countermeasures*

Privacy-Enhancing Technologies: The use of privacy-enhancing technologies such as VPNs, encrypted messaging services, and more secure forms of digital communication can become more widespread as individuals seek to protect their privacy from state surveillance.

Legal and Activist Resistance: Legal challenges to surveillance programs and activism focused on privacy rights can also increase. Civil liberties organizations might lead efforts to challenge invasive laws and educate the public on their rights and ways to protect their privacy.

### *Long-Term Cultural Shifts*

Cultural Shift Towards Privacy Advocacy: In response to increased surveillance, there could be a cultural shift that places greater value on privacy, leading to stronger public advocacy for privacy rights and reforms.

Changes in Legislation and Policy: Sustained public pressure and shifting cultural norms could eventually lead to changes in legislation and policy that restore some privacy protections and curb government surveillance.

In Essence, The increase in government surveillance and the reduction in privacy rights under a more authoritarian regime could significantly alter the daily lives of average Privileged White Americans, along with all other citizens. These changes can affect everything from personal behaviors and social interactions to mental health and societal cohesion. It underscores the need for vigilance, resistance, and advocacy to protect personal freedoms and ensure that privacy rights are upheld.

# Legal Insecurity: Erosion of Judicial Protections under Authoritarian Rule

In an authoritarian regime, the balance of power often shifts significantly toward the executive branch, with the judiciary weakened or manipulated to align with the executive's interests. This shift can erode legal protections, making the law less a tool for justice and more a mechanism for maintaining power. For average Privileged White Americans, traditionally perceived as part of a protected majority, this new reality could expose them to unexpected legal vulnerabilities.

### *Weakening of the Judiciary*

Undermining Judicial Independence: Authoritarian leaders may take steps to undermine the independence of the judiciary, such as appointing judges based on loyalty rather than merit, influencing legal decisions, or curbing the courts' power to check other branches of government. This compromises the judiciary's role as an unbiased arbiter of legal disputes.

Manipulation of Legal Processes: There might be an increase in the manipulation of legal processes to serve political ends. Laws could be selectively enforced, or legal proceedings might be skewed to disadvantage political or ideological opponents, which can include average citizens who oppose or do not support the regime.

## Expansion of Executive Powers

Broad Executive Authorities: With expanded powers, the executive may enact laws, change policies, and make decisions without adequate legislative review or judicial oversight. This can include declaring states of emergency that extend executive powers beyond their normal limits, impacting citizens' rights and freedoms.

Arbitrary Decision-Making: The concentration of power often leads to arbitrary decision-making. Without the checks and balances typically provided by a strong judiciary, executive decisions can go unchecked, leading to abuses of power that can affect ordinary citizens' lives.

## Impact on Legal Protections

Erosion of Civil Liberties: Fundamental civil liberties, such as the freedom of speech, right to privacy, and protection from unreasonable searches and seizures, can be eroded under authoritarian regimes. This erosion can make average citizens, including Privileged White Americans, more vulnerable to surveillance, censorship, and arbitrary arrests.

Decreased Legal Recourse: As legal institutions weaken, the ability of individuals to challenge unjust laws or governmental actions diminishes. This lack of recourse can leave citizens feeling powerless and vulnerable to exploitation or persecution.

## Vulnerability to Legal Injustices

Arbitrary Law Enforcement: Average citizens might find themselves subject to arbitrary law enforcement practices. This could include being targeted for minor infractions or activities that were previously ignored or deemed legal, as the law becomes a more flexible tool in the hands of the authorities.

Legal Uncertainty: The unpredictability of an authoritarian legal system can lead to a general sense of insecurity. Laws may change frequently, be applied inconsistently, or be interpreted in ways that favor the regime, making it difficult for average citizens to navigate their legal obligations and rights.

## Social and Economic Consequences

Impact on Business and Employment: Legal insecurity can stifle economic activity and innovation. Businesses may be hesitant to invest or expand in an unpredictable legal environment, potentially leading to job losses and economic decline, which affects all sectors of society, including average Privileged White Americans.

Deterioration of Social Trust: As the legal system becomes viewed as an instrument of oppression rather than justice, social trust deteriorates. This can lead to a less cooperative society, where individuals are more likely to act in self-interest or out of fear rather than for the common good.

## Strategies for Restoration and Advocacy

Legal Advocacy and Public Pressure: Building coalitions to advocate for judicial independence and the restoration of legal checks on executive power is crucial. Public awareness campaigns can educate citizens on the importance of a balanced government and the rule of law.

Support for Legal Reform Movements: Supporting movements and organizations dedicated to legal reform and the protection of civil liberties can help push back against the erosion of legal standards and practices.

In Essence The potential weakening of the judiciary and the expansion of executive powers in an authoritarian regime can lead to significant legal insecurity for all citizens, including average Privileged White Americans. This shift not only challenges the fairness and integrity of the legal system but also affects every aspect of civic life, underscoring the importance of vigilant, informed, and active engagement in democratic processes to safeguard legal protections.

# Chapter 6: Long-Term Risks

# Threats to Democracy: The Ripple Effects on Stability and Security

The breakdown of democratic norms can precipitate a wide range of destabilizing effects across society, disrupting the stability that many, including Privileged White Americans, may have previously taken for granted. As these foundational elements of governance erode, the consequences can extend far beyond the political arena, affecting economic conditions, social cohesion, and even personal security. This section explores how the deterioration of democracy might manifest in economic downturns, political instability, and potential conflicts and how these changes could impact the daily lives and well-being of Privileged White Americans.

## *Economic Instability*

Investor Confidence and Market Reactions: The onset of political instability can lead to a decline in investor confidence, which might result in stock market volatility and reduced foreign investment. Economic downturns often follow as businesses curtail operations or withhold investment in uncertain regulatory and political climates.

Job Security and Unemployment: Economic slowdowns, driven by reduced investment and consumer confidence, can lead to higher unemployment rates. Job security becomes precarious, affecting sectors across the board, from blue-collar industries to white-collar professions predominantly occupied by Privileged White Americans.

## *Political Instability*

Governmental Turnover and Policy Inconsistency: As democratic norms erode, government turnover can become more frequent and erratic, whether through electoral upheavals or more authoritarian measures like purges and unilateral executive actions. This inconsistency in leadership can lead to erratic policies that further destabilize the economy and social order.

Loss of International Standing: Political instability can diminish a country's standing on the global stage, affecting everything from international trade agreements to foreign policy. For individuals, this could mean a reduction in the global influence that they might have previously enjoyed or taken for granted.

## Social Unrest and Conflicts

Increase in Social Unrest: As different groups vie for power or protest against authoritarian measures, incidents of social unrest, including protests, strikes, and riots, can increase. This unrest can disrupt daily life, making public spaces feel unsafe and unpredictable.

Polarization and Violence: Political and social polarization might escalate into violence, particularly if extremist groups gain prominence or if the state employs heavy-handed tactics to suppress dissent. Such environments can lead to communal conflicts, affecting all members of society, including Privileged White Americans.

## Personal and Community Impact

Sense of Security: The combined effects of economic downturns, political instability, and social unrest can severely impact personal security and well-being. The anxiety and stress associated with these conditions can affect mental health, reduce the quality of life, and lead to a pervasive sense of insecurity.

Community Cohesion: As trust in democratic institutions and processes erodes, so too might the social fabric of communities. Divisions can deepen, and the cooperative spirit necessary for communal projects and social harmony can deteriorate, leaving communities fractured and less resilient in the face of challenges.

## Mitigation Strategies

Civic Engagement and Education: Reinforcing the importance of civic engagement and promoting education about democratic values are crucial steps in mitigating the decline of democratic norms. Active participation in local and national governance and informed voting can help stem the tide of authoritarianism.

Support for Democratic Institutions: Supporting and strengthening institutions that uphold democratic principles, such as independent media, judicial systems, and electoral bodies, is essential for maintaining democratic governance and political stability.

## Building Resilience

Economic Diversification: Encouraging economic diversification and innovation can buffer against the economic shocks that political instability might bring. Supporting small businesses, investing in technology, and promoting sustainable practices can help create a more resilient economy.

Community Solidarity Initiatives: Fostering initiatives that build community solidarity and promote inclusive dialogue can help bridge divides and reinforce social cohesion in the face of rising tensions.

In Essence The breakdown of democratic norms poses significant risks to the stability and security that many Privileged White Americans have come to expect. Addressing these threats requires a proactive and concerted effort to bolster democratic practices, protect economic and social stability, and ensure a secure environment for all citizens. By engaging actively in democratic processes and supporting policies that enhance stability and inclusivity, individuals can help safeguard their communities and their well-being against the disruptions that accompany the erosion of democracy.

# Erosion of Legal Protections: Vulnerability in an Authoritarian Regime

The shift towards authoritarianism often brings with it a significant erosion of legal protections, affecting all strata of society, including those previously insulated by privilege. As the rule of law becomes subject to the whims of those in power, the very fabric of legal security can unravel, leaving even privileged individuals vulnerable to arbitrary decisions. This section explores the mechanisms of this erosion, its impact on privileged communities, and the broader implications for the rule of law.

## Undermining Judicial Independence

Political Interference: One of the first steps in an authoritarian shift is often the undermining of judicial independence. This can occur through political interference, where judges are appointed based on loyalty rather than merit, or where political pressures dictate judicial decisions.

Compromised Legal Integrity: As the judiciary becomes a tool of the executive, the integrity of legal judgments can be compromised. Laws may be interpreted or applied in ways that serve the interests of those in power rather than reflecting justice or precedent.

## Arbitrary Application of the Law

Selective Enforcement: Authoritarian regimes may enforce laws selectively to benefit allies and penalize opponents. This selective enforcement can lead privileged individuals who fall out of favor to suddenly find themselves at the mercy of laws that were previously unenforced or applied with leniency.

Legal Manipulation: Laws may be manipulated or newly enacted to consolidate power, suppress dissent, or remove obstacles to authoritarian objectives. This manipulation can lead to sudden changes in the legal landscape, catching individuals unprepared and unprotected.

## Loss of Legal Protections

Erosion of Property Rights: In authoritarian regimes, property rights can become highly conditional. Confiscations or expropriations might occur with little to no compensation, especially if individuals are perceived as threats to the regime.

Diminished Personal Liberties: Rights such as privacy, free speech, and due process can be heavily curtailed. Privileged individuals might find that their ability to speak out or protect their personal information is significantly reduced without the safeguards previously provided by a robust legal system.

## *Implications for Privileged Individuals*

Vulnerability to Political Shifts: As legal protections become contingent on political favor, privileged individuals may find their security is volatile and directly tied to their relationship with ruling powers. Loss of favor could result in rapid legal and personal repercussions.

Reduced Influence: Previously, privileged individuals might have leveraged their status to navigate or even manipulate legal outcomes. However, under a strong authoritarian regime, this influence can diminish unless directly aligned with the powers that be.

## *Broader Societal Impact*

Culture of Fear and Compliance: The erosion of legal protections contributes to a culture of fear and compliance. As people see that not even privileged individuals are safe from arbitrary legal actions, the incentive to conform increases, and the genuine rule of law deteriorates.

Legal Cynicism: A pervasive distrust in the fairness and effectiveness of the legal system can develop, undermining civic engagement and the public's willingness to seek legal redress. This cynicism can stifle social and economic innovation as the legal environment becomes seen as unpredictable and unjust.

## *Strategies for Restoration and Resistance*

International Legal Support: Leveraging international legal standards and seeking support from international bodies can provide some measure of protection or redress against authoritarian practices.

Advocacy and Legal Reform: Building coalitions for legal reform and advocating for the restoration of judicial independence are critical. These efforts can help resist the erosion of legal protections and promote a recommitment to the rule of law.

In Essence, The erosion of legal protections in an authoritarian regime represents a profound shift that affects everyone, including those who might once have felt secure due to their social or economic status. Recognizing the interconnectedness of legal security for all segments of society is crucial in mobilizing effective resistance and advocating for a restoration of genuine rule of law principles.

# Concentration of Power: Erosion of Influence Among the Privileged

The concentration of power within a small elite or under a single authoritarian leader is a hallmark of many authoritarian regimes. Initially, broader privileged classes may support or tolerate this consolidation in the hope of maintaining their status and influence. However, as power becomes increasingly centralized, these same groups might find themselves unexpectedly marginalized from decision-making processes. This section explores the dynamics of power concentration, its impact on the privileged, and the broader implications for governance and social structure.

## *Mechanisms of Power Concentration*

Centralization in Leadership: Authoritarian regimes often centralize power around a single leader or a small group of elites. This centralization can involve the elimination of checks and balances, the merging of executive powers with legislative authorities, and the curtailment of judicial independence.

Suppression of Alternative Power Centers: To solidify their control, authoritarian leaders might systematically dismantle or weaken institutions that could serve as centers of alternative power, such as independent media, academia, and even sectors of the economy that enjoy a degree of autonomy.

## *Impact on the Privileged Classes*

Loss of Political Influence: As power is centralized, the broader privileged class may find that their traditional avenues for influence, such as lobbying, political contributions, or social connections, become less effective. The new power structure might not value these contributions or might view the privileged class as a potential threat to their authority.

Exclusion from Elite Circles: Even within privileged groups, a new elite may emerge that is closely aligned with the authoritarian leader. This can lead to stratification within the upper echelons of society, where only a select few enjoy the benefits of proximity to power.

## Risks of Marginalization

Arbitrary Decision-Making: With fewer checks on their power, authoritarian leaders can make decisions that are unpredictable and self-serving. Privileged individuals used to a stable rule of law might find themselves at the mercy of these whimsical decisions.

Confiscation and Seizure: In extreme cases, the assets and properties of previously privileged individuals can be confiscated or seized under various pretexts, often with little legal recourse or justification, other than the leader's discretion.

## Social and Economic Consequences

Weakening of Social Networks: The traditional social networks through which the privileged exerted influence can become disrupted or controlled by the state. This can lead to a breakdown in the informal systems of support and exchange that previously benefited these groups.

Economic Uncertainty: The economic landscape may become unpredictable as policies are dictated by the needs or desires of the ruling elite rather than sound economic principles. This can deter investment, stifle economic growth, and ultimately impact the wealth and stability of the privileged class.

## Strategies for Adaptation and Resistance

Building New Alliances: To regain influence, members of the privileged class may need to form new alliances, possibly with other marginalized groups or international partners, to challenge the concentration of power.

Advocacy for Institutional Strengthening: Advocating for the strengthening and independence of institutions is crucial. This includes supporting the rule of law, independent judiciary, and free press as bulwarks against the arbitrary concentration of power.

### *Legal and International Recourse*

Legal Challenges: Utilizing legal channels, both domestically and internationally, can provide a means to contest the erosion of rights and properties.

International Pressure and Sanctions: Leveraging international pressure and potential sanctions can be an effective strategy for privileged groups to challenge authoritarian practices and advocate for a return to more democratic governance structures.

In Essence The concentration of power in authoritarian regimes represents a significant challenge not just to the disenfranchised but also to the traditionally privileged classes. As these individuals find themselves excluded from power and influence, the need for strategic adaptation becomes critical. Understanding the dynamics of power concentration and actively participating in efforts to decentralize authority can help mitigate the risks associated with authoritarian rule and promote a more equitable and democratic distribution of power.

# Economic Instability: Long-Term Consequences of Unchecked Policies

While deregulation and tax cuts can present immediate financial advantages to the wealthy, including Privileged White Americans, the long-term economic consequences of these policies can be significantly destabilizing. Unchecked economic policies that favor the upper echelons of society at the expense of broader economic stability can lead to market crashes, exacerbated inequality, and ensuing social unrest. This section explores how such economic strategies might initially seem beneficial. Still, it could ultimately jeopardize the very wealth and security they aim to enhance.

## *Short-Term Gains vs. Long-Term Risks*

Initial Economic Boost: Deregulation and tax cuts can stimulate economic activity by increasing disposable income for the wealthy and reducing operational costs for businesses. This can lead to short-term increases in investment and consumption that drive economic growth.

Unsustainable Growth and Bubbles: Over time, these policies can contribute to economic bubbles as markets overheat. The lack of regulation in critical sectors like banking and real estate can lead to risky investments and speculative behavior, setting the stage for financial crises.

## *Market Crashes and Economic Cycles*

Volatility and Crashes: With reduced oversight and unchecked speculation, financial markets can become highly volatile. The eventual bursting of bubbles, as seen in the 2008 financial crisis, can lead to severe market crashes that wipe out vast amounts of wealth and destabilize the global economy.

Recessions: Economic downturns and recessions often follow these crashes, leading to widespread unemployment, reduced consumer spending, and a slow recovery process that can take years, impacting all economic classes, including the wealthy.

## *Increased Economic Inequality*

Wealth Concentration: While the wealthy may benefit disproportionately from deregulation and tax cuts, such policies often do little to lift the economic prospects of the middle and lower classes. Over time, this leads to increased economic inequality, with wealth becoming increasingly concentrated at the top.

Reduced Economic Mobility: As inequality widens, economic mobility decreases. The lack of reinvestment in public goods such as education, healthcare, and infrastructure, typically funded through taxes, can stifle opportunities for the broader population, further entrenching economic disparities.

## Social Unrest and Instability

Rising Discontent: As the gap between the wealthy and the rest of society widens, discontent and frustration can grow among those who feel left behind. This can manifest in increased social unrest, protests, and demands for economic reform.

Impact on Public Safety: Prolonged periods of economic instability and social unrest can lead to a deterioration in public safety. Crime rates may increase, and social order can be threatened, affecting the quality of life for all, including privileged communities.

## Implications for Policy and Governance

Calls for Regulatory Reforms: In response to economic crises and social pressures, there can be significant public demand for increased regulation and more progressive taxation policies. Such shifts can alter the economic landscape, potentially rolling back previous advantages enjoyed by the wealthy.

Political Shifts: Economic instability can lead to political shifts, with new leaders or parties coming to power on platforms that promise to address inequality and regulate industries more stringently. These changes can further impact the economic strategies that privileged groups might rely on.

## Strategies for Mitigation

Balanced Economic Policies: Encouraging policies that strike a balance between stimulating economic growth and preventing excessive risk and inequality is crucial. This might include more nuanced approaches to taxation and regulation that promote long-term stability.

Investment in Social Programs: Investing in comprehensive social programs can help mitigate the impacts of economic downturns and promote a more stable and productive society. These investments benefit all social strata, including the privileged, by fostering a more secure and resilient economy.

In Essence While deregulation and tax cuts might initially seem to favor the economic interests of Privileged White Americans, the long-term consequences of these policies can lead to significant economic instability. Market crashes, increased inequality, and social unrest not only threaten the economic framework but also the very security and stability of the society in which the privileged exist. Recognizing and addressing the potential downsides of these economic strategies is essential for ensuring sustainable growth and social harmony.

# Chapter 7: Global Consequences

# Isolation: The Global Consequences of Authoritarianism in the U.S.

A shift towards authoritarianism in the United States could have significant repercussions beyond its borders, affecting the country's international standing and relationships. This shift could lead to economic and diplomatic isolation, with profound impacts on trade, travel, and global cooperation. Such changes would not only alter the nation's role on the world stage but also directly affect the daily lives of Privileged White Americans, particularly those whose livelihoods, travel habits, or business operations depend on international connections.

## *Deterioration of International Relations*

Diplomatic Fallout: As the U.S. potentially adopts more inward-looking and unilateral policies under an authoritarian regime, it may face strained relationships with traditional allies and international partners. Disagreements over human rights, governance standards, and international law could lead to diplomatic stand-offs or the severance of longstanding partnerships.

Withdrawal from International Agreements: A withdrawal from international agreements and institutions, such as climate accords, trade deals, or defense pacts, could further isolate the U.S. on the global stage. This would not only diminish its influence but also impact the global systems that rely on the country's leadership and participation.

## *Economic Consequences*

Impact on Trade: Economic isolation could result from tariffs, trade wars, or sanctions, either imposed by the U.S. or in response by other nations. Such economic measures could disrupt international trade networks that industries and consumers in the U.S. rely on, leading to increased costs and reduced availability of goods.

Foreign Investment and Markets: The perception of the U.S. as an unstable or risky partner could deter foreign investment. American businesses operating abroad might face increased scrutiny, barriers, and even expulsion from foreign markets, affecting global operations and profits.

## Effects on Travel and Mobility

Travel Restrictions: The imposition of travel restrictions, both on Americans traveling abroad and on international visitors to the U.S., could become more common. This might include stricter visa requirements, reduced flight connectivity, or travel bans, complicating personal and business travel.

International Isolation in Personal Lives: For Privileged White Americans accustomed to traveling or living abroad, increased global isolation could limit opportunities for international education, employment, and cultural exchange, reducing their global mobility and exposure.

## Impact on Globalized Industries

Supply Chain Disruptions: Industries that rely on global supply chains could encounter significant disruptions. Restrictions or tariffs on imported materials and goods could lead to production delays, increased costs, and competitive disadvantages on the global market.

Technology and Innovation: In fields such as technology and pharmaceuticals, where innovation often relies on international collaboration, isolation could hinder research and development efforts, putting American companies at a disadvantage.

## Social and Cultural Impacts

Cultural Exchange and Influence: A more isolated U.S. might see a reduction in cultural exchange programs, international student enrollments, and participation in international arts and sports events, leading to a cultural withdrawal that could impoverish the social and cultural life of Americans.

Perceptions and Stereotypes: Internationally, Americans might be viewed through the lens of their government's policies, potentially leading to stereotypes and biases that affect personal and professional interactions abroad.

### *Mitigation and Adaptation Strategies*

Diplomatic Engagement: Encouraging the government to maintain or re-establish diplomatic and economic ties can help mitigate isolation. Advocacy for engagement rather than withdrawal can preserve important international relationships.

Local and State Level International Initiatives: Local and state governments can pursue their own international collaborations and trade initiatives to circumvent federal limitations, maintaining global connections and cultural exchanges.

In Essence, The potential move towards authoritarianism and resulting isolation could profoundly impact the U.S.'s international standing and the daily lives of its citizens, including Privileged White Americans reliant on global interactions. The economic, social, and cultural ramifications necessitate a proactive approach to maintaining international relationships and commitments, ensuring that the U.S. remains a connected and responsible global player.

# Loss of Global Prestige: Consequences of an Authoritarian Shift in the U.S.

A shift towards authoritarianism in the United States can significantly impact its global prestige and influence, altering how the nation is perceived and engaged on the international stage. For Privileged White Americans, particularly those involved in international business, travel, or cultural exchanges, these changes could have profound personal and professional repercussions. This section explores the potential decline in U.S. global standing due to authoritarian policies and the specific impacts on its citizens' international activities.

## *Decline in Diplomatic Influence*

Weakening of Alliances and Partnerships: As the U.S. adopts more authoritarian practices, its traditional allies may distance themselves, weakening long-standing diplomatic ties. This erosion of alliances could diminish the U.S.'s ability to influence global politics and economic agreements.

Reduced Participation in International Organizations: A withdrawal or reduced engagement from international organizations like the UN, WTO, or NATO could further isolate the U.S. and limit its role in global governance, affecting international norms and policies that have long been favorable to American interests.

## *Economic Repercussions*

Trade Sanctions and Retaliations: Authoritarian policies might provoke trade sanctions from other countries, which could impact American businesses operating abroad. Privileged White Americans who own or invest in these businesses could see their overseas operations suffer due to increased tariffs, import restrictions, or outright bans.

Impact on Foreign Investments: As global perceptions of the U.S. shift, foreign entities might be less inclined to invest in American markets or start joint ventures. This retreat could affect the broader economy, impacting job creation and innovation, sectors where privileged individuals often have significant stakes.

## *Travel and Cultural Exchange Limitations*

Visa Restrictions and Travel Bans: In response to U.S. policies, other countries might impose visa restrictions or travel bans on American citizens, complicating or even blocking travel opportunities for business, tourism, or cultural activities.

Cultural Isolation: Reduced cultural exchange due to strained international relations can lead to a decline in global cultural influence. Privileged White

Americans involved in cultural industries such as art, music, academia, or entertainment might find fewer opportunities for international collaboration and audience reach.

## Social and Personal Impacts

Stigmatization Abroad: Individuals from the U.S. might encounter stigmatization or hostility while abroad due to their nation's political stance. This can affect personal safety, ease of travel, and the ability to form international connections.

Loss of Global Mobility and Prestige: A decline in the U.S.'s reputation can affect the prestige and mobility of its citizens, including those who previously enjoyed an elevated status due to their country's perceived leadership in democracy and freedom.

## Implications for Global Business Operations

Operational Challenges: Companies with global supply chains or markets might face operational challenges, including disruptions in supply chains, increased costs of doing business, and potential expropriation or regulatory challenges in foreign jurisdictions.

Reputational Risks: Businesses associated with a country perceived as authoritarian might suffer reputational damage, affecting their brand value and customer base, particularly in regions that value democratic governance.

## Strategies for Mitigation

Enhanced Public Diplomacy: individuals and businesses can engage in public diplomacy efforts, emphasizing American values of innovation, reliability, and quality in their international dealings. To counteract these negative perceptions,

Diversification of Markets and Alliances: Diversifying business operations and building new alliances in less affected regions or countries can help mitigate some of the geopolitical risks associated with U.S. policy shifts.

In Essence, The potential move towards authoritarianism in the U.S. could significantly impact its global standing, affecting not just diplomatic and economic relations but also the personal and professional lives of its privileged citizens. The challenges posed by this shift necessitate proactive strategies to maintain international relationships, protect global business interests, and preserve cultural exchanges, ensuring that Privileged White Americans can continue to engage effectively on the global stage despite potential national policy shifts.

# Isolation and Decline in Opportunities: Global Repercussions of U.S. Shifts

As the United States potentially shifts towards more authoritarian practices, its perception on the global stage could undergo significant changes, leading to diplomatic and economic isolation. This isolation can manifest in reduced opportunities not only for the country at large but specifically for Privileged White Americans, who may have previously enjoyed a broad spectrum of international benefits in business, education, and lifestyle.

## *Changes in Global Perception*

Altered International Image: The image of the U.S. as a beacon of democracy and a stable partner could be tarnished if it veers toward authoritarianism. This shift may lead international observers and partners to reassess their relationships with the U.S., perceiving it as a less reliable or desirable ally.

Impact on Soft Power: The soft power derived from cultural influence, political values, and diplomatic relations could wane, affecting everything from cultural exports to international policy influence.

## *Economic and Business Impact*

Reduced International Business Opportunities: As the U.S. faces potential sanctions or trade barriers in response to its policies, Privileged White Americans involved in international business might find lucrative markets becoming restrictive or inaccessible. This could lead to decreased revenue and growth opportunities for businesses reliant on global supply chains or markets.

Investment Challenges: Foreign investments might decline as international investors seek more stable and democratic environments. This reduction could affect real estate, technology, manufacturing, and other sectors where Privileged White Americans traditionally hold significant interests.

## Educational and Cultural Exchanges

Impact on International Education: Students and academics might face hurdles in participating in global educational exchanges. Visa restrictions, reduced funding, or partner institutions' hesitancy to engage with American entities could limit opportunities for studying abroad or collaborating on international research.

Cultural Isolation: The U.S. might see a decline in its cultural influence, with fewer opportunities to showcase American arts, music, and literature on the global stage. This isolation could also limit the cultural enrichment that comes from engaging with diverse international communities.

## Lifestyle and Travel Restrictions

Travel Limitations: Privileged White Americans accustomed to frequent travel might encounter new visa requirements, increased scrutiny at borders, or outright bans from certain countries. These changes could complicate or discourage international travel for business or leisure.

Decreased Quality of Life: The cosmopolitan lifestyle that many privileged Americans enjoy, characterized by global travel, luxury goods, and international social events, could be curtailed. This could lead to a perceived decrease in quality of life and global connectivity.

## Social and Professional Networks

Contraction of Professional Networks: Professional networks that span borders could shrink or become less effective as other nationals might be wary of too close an association with American businesses or professionals.

Social Stigma: Socially Privileged White Americans might encounter a stigma attached to their country's political stance, impacting personal relationships and social interactions in international settings.

## *Mitigation and Adaptation Strategies*

Enhancing International Relations: Individuals and businesses can work to enhance their international relationships through independent branding, emphasizing values such as sustainability, ethical practices, and corporate social responsibility that may contrast with their home country's authoritarian image.

Diversification of Markets and Alliances: Diversifying business and educational ties beyond traditional allies to include emerging markets or neutral countries could help mitigate some of the negative impacts of U.S. isolation.

In Essence The potential isolation of the U.S. in response to authoritarian shifts could significantly impact Privileged White Americans, reducing their international business, educational, and lifestyle opportunities. The broader implications for their social and economic prospects highlight the need for proactive strategies that safeguard global relationships and maintain international engagement in a changing geopolitical landscape.

# Chapter 8: Impact on Freedom and Privacy

# Concentration of Power: Implications for Local Governance and Representation

The concentration of power at the national level, particularly within a centralized federal government, can significantly impact the political dynamics and governance at local and state levels. For average Privileged White Americans, this centralization may manifest as a diminishing influence and representation in their local and state governments. This section explores how the consolidation of power affects local governance, the erosion of local autonomy, and the broader implications for democratic participation.

## *Erosion of Local Autonomy*

Centralization of Decision-Making: As power consolidates at the federal level, decisions that were traditionally made by local or state governments may increasingly be dictated by national authorities. This shift can sideline local needs and priorities, with policies being implemented that may not align with local constituents' preferences.

Preemption of Local Laws: Federal authorities may begin to preempt local laws more frequently, overriding state and local regulations that conflict with national agendas. This could involve critical areas such as environmental regulations, labor laws, and civil rights protections, where local communities previously had more say.

## *Reduced Local Representation and Influence*

Diminished Voice in Governance: With more decisions being made at the national level, average Privileged White Americans might feel that their ability to influence governance through local elections and engagements is significantly reduced. This perception can lead to increased political disengagement and cynicism regarding the efficacy of their participation.

Standardization of Policies: Centralized decision-making might lead to a one-size-fits-all approach in policy-making, where diverse local conditions and preferences are not adequately considered. This standardization can be particularly frustrating for local populations that have distinct social, economic, or environmental conditions.

## *Impact on Local Governance Structures*

Weakening of Local Institutions: As the federal government strengthens its grip, local institutions such as city councils, school boards, and other local bodies may find their powers curtailed. This weakening can impact their ability to serve the specific needs of their communities effectively.

Resource Allocation: There may be a redistribution of resources that favors national priorities over local needs. This can result in local projects and services suffering from underfunding, affecting everything from infrastructure maintenance to public school resources.

## *Public Response and Sentiment*

Feelings of Alienation: The distance between the government and the governed can grow, leading to feelings of alienation among average citizens. When people do not see their local realities and challenges reflected in national policymaking, it can diminish their trust and confidence in the government.

Increase in Local Activism: In response to perceived overreach by the federal government, there might be a resurgence in local activism. Communities may band together to demand more autonomy and push back against federal policies that they see as intrusive or detrimental to local interests.

## *Strategies for Reasserting Local Control*

Strengthening State and Local Advocacy: Communities can strengthen their state and local advocacy efforts, ensuring that their representatives are committed to defending local autonomy against federal overreach.

Engagement in Local Politics: Encouraging greater participation in local politics can help ensure that local governments reflect the will and interests of their constituents. This includes voting in local elections, participating in town halls, and supporting local candidates who advocate for decentralization of power.

### *Legal Challenges and Reforms*

Legal Recourse: States and local governments might pursue legal challenges against federal actions that they deem overreach, asserting their rights in court to maintain local governance powers.

Legislative Reforms: Advocating for legislative reforms that clearly delineate the powers of local versus federal government can help prevent conflicts and ensure a more balanced distribution of governance responsibilities.

In Essence As power becomes more concentrated in the hands of the few at the federal level, the impact on local and state governance can be profound, affecting how average Privileged White Americans and, indeed, all citizens experience and interact with their government. The erosion of local autonomy not only challenges the principles of federalism but also diminishes the democratic engagement and representation of local communities. Strengthening local governance and advocacy is crucial in maintaining a balanced power distribution that respects local needs and priorities.

# Increased Surveillance: Implications for All Citizens in an Authoritarian State

In an authoritarian regime, the expansion of state surveillance is often justified as a necessary measure for national security and maintaining social order. However, such surveillance can extend across all societal strata, including the wealthy and influential, who might have previously felt immune due to their status. This section explores the reasons behind widespread surveillance, how it affects privileged individuals, and the broader implications for privacy and personal freedom.

### *Rationale for Expanded Surveillance*

Control and Suppression: Authoritarian governments often aim to suppress any potential threats to their power, including dissent from influential citizens. Surveillance becomes a tool to monitor and preempt opposition by keeping tabs on everyone's activities, communications, and movements.

Information Gathering: Collecting data on citizens, including those from upper social echelons, allows the government to build comprehensive profiles that could be used to leverage compliance or silence through blackmail or coercion.

## Mechanisms of Surveillance

Digital Monitoring: This could include tapping of phone calls, interception of emails, and scrutiny of social media activities. Advanced algorithms and data mining techniques might be employed to analyze patterns and predict behaviors of all citizens, irrespective of their social status.

Physical Surveillance: CCTV cameras, facial recognition technology, and even drones can be used in public and private spaces to monitor the movements of influential individuals as closely as those of average citizens.

## Impact on Privileged Individuals

Loss of Privacy: Wealthy and influential individuals might find that their financial transactions, business dealings, and personal interactions are as monitored as those of any other citizen. This loss of privacy can be particularly alarming for those who previously believed their status afforded them protection.

Vulnerability to State Intervention: With detailed surveillance, the state gains the upper hand and can intervene or exert pressure if a privileged individual's actions are perceived as contrary to the interests of those in power.

## Social and Psychological Effects

Erosion of Trust: Knowing that they are subject to surveillance can lead to an erosion of trust among community members, business partners, and even within families. This distrust can permeate all levels of society, creating an atmosphere of fear and suspicion.

Self-Censorship: The knowledge of being watched might lead privileged individuals to self-censor, avoiding not just overt criticism of the government but also any engagements that could be construed as dissent.

## Broader Implications for Society

Chilling Effect on Innovation: Surveillance can stifle creativity and innovation, as people become less likely to take risks or explore novel ideas if they feel that they are constantly being monitored.

Normalization of Surveillance: Over time, the acceptance of surveillance as a part of daily life can lead to the normalization of privacy invasions, permanently altering societal expectations about personal freedom and autonomy.

## Resistance and Mitigation Strategies

Legal Challenges: Where possible, legal avenues might be pursued to challenge the extent and legality of surveillance. However, this cannot be easy in an authoritarian context.

Technological Countermeasures: The use of encrypted communication tools, VPNs, and other privacy-enhancing technologies can provide some level of protection against surveillance.

Advocacy and Alliance Building: Building alliances with other affected groups to advocate for privacy rights and restrictions on government surveillance can be an effective strategy, though it carries risks in an authoritarian regime.

In Essence In an authoritarian state, increased surveillance affects everyone, including those who are privileged. The comprehensive monitoring of all citizens' activities represents a significant intrusion into personal life. It has far-reaching consequences for individual freedoms and societal dynamics. Recognizing these impacts is crucial for any resistance efforts, as well as for understanding the full scope of changes to personal and public life under increased state surveillance.

# Restricted Freedom of Expression: The Impact on Privileged Individuals

In authoritarian regimes, the suppression of free speech and expression is a common tactic used to control and maintain power. Initially, privileged individuals may feel insulated from these restrictions, particularly if they align with or support the regime. However, as the authoritarian grip tightens, these individuals might discover that their freedom to speak and express dissent is equally curtailed, especially if they begin to diverge from or criticize the government. This section explores the dynamics of restricted freedom of expression, its impact on privileged individuals, and the broader implications for society.

## *Mechanisms of Suppressing Free Expression*

Legislative Restrictions: Authoritarian governments often enact laws that restrict speech under the guise of protecting national security, maintaining public order, or preserving national unity. These laws can be broadly interpreted to stifle any form of criticism or dissent.

Censorship and Media Control: Control over the media is tightened, with publications, broadcasts, and online content being closely monitored and censored. Privileged individuals who own media outlets or have influence in cultural spheres may find themselves particularly targeted to ensure that their platforms do not become avenues for anti-government rhetoric.

## *Impact on Privileged Individuals*

Personal and Professional Risks: Those in privileged positions may face personal and professional repercussions if they express views that are contrary to authoritarian policies. This could include social ostracism, professional setbacks, or even legal actions.

Self-Censorship: Knowing the potential consequences, many may choose to self-censor, avoiding any public or private expressions that could be deemed critical of the state. This self-censorship stifles genuine expression and can lead to intellectual stagnation.

## Consequences for Intellectual and Cultural Growth

Stifling of Intellectual Debate: The lack of freedom to express diverse opinions and to debate openly leads to a decline in intellectual vigor and critical thinking within society. Academic institutions and think tanks may limit their scope of research and discussion to avoid crossing red lines.

Cultural Homogenization: In cultural arenas, the arts, literature, and public performances may lose their edge, becoming tools for propaganda rather than expressions of human experience and creativity. This homogenization restricts cultural development and diminishes the society's ability to reflect on itself and evolve.

## Broader Societal Implications

Erosion of Public Discourse: As the space for open dialogue shrinks, the quality of public discourse deteriorates. Without the ability to challenge ideas, discuss solutions, and voice grievances, the development of public policy suffers, and societal progress stalls.

Increase in Underground Movements: The suppression of legitimate avenues for expression can lead to the rise of underground movements. While these can be vibrant hubs of resistance, they also risk further governmental crackdowns, leading to cycles of repression and dissent.

## Strategies for Resistance and Adaptation

Promotion of Alternative Communication Channels: Privileged individuals can support or establish alternative platforms for expression, such as underground publications, private salons, or encrypted digital forums, where free discourse can continue.

International Advocacy: Leveraging international connections to advocate for freedom of expression can provide some protection and a broader platform for dissent. International forums and human rights organizations can be pivotal in applying pressure on authoritarian regimes.

## *Legal and Social Advocacy*

Legal Defense Initiatives: Supporting legal defense initiatives that challenge restrictive laws and defend those persecuted for their expressions can help maintain a semblance of the rule of law.

Solidarity Networks: Building solidarity networks among like-minded individuals and groups can help sustain morale and provide a collective front against authoritarian measures. These networks can also facilitate mutual aid, including legal and financial support.

In Essence The restriction of freedom of expression under authoritarian regimes represents a critical loss for society, including for those initially aligned with the regime. For privileged individuals, experiencing this suppression firsthand can be both a wake-up call and a catalyst for action. Recognizing the importance of free expression for societal health and dynamism is crucial for any efforts to resist authoritarian encroachments and to foster a vibrant, open society.

# Chapter 9: IMoral and Ethical Considerations

# Complicity in Injustice: Ethical Dilemmas Among Privileged White Americans

As an authoritarian regime consolidates power, Privileged White Americans who initially may have supported or benefited from the regime could face profound ethical dilemmas. The realization of their complicity in perpetuating injustices and inequalities can lead to internal conflicts, guilt, and a deep-seated crisis of conscience. This exploration delves into the psychological and moral challenges that arise when privileged individuals confront their role in sustaining an oppressive system and the potential pathways for moral redemption and social responsibility.

## *Realization of Complicity*

Awareness of Injustice: As the authoritarian regime's policies become more overtly oppressive, the evidence of human rights abuses, discrimination, and suppression of dissent can become undeniable. Privileged individuals may begin to see the direct and indirect consequences of their support for the regime.

Reflection on Personal Benefit: There may be a stark realization that their comfort, security, and economic advantages have been gained at the expense of others' freedoms and well-being. This awareness can be particularly jarring for those who previously viewed themselves as fair, ethical, or neutral.

## *Moral and Ethical Implications*

Internal Moral Conflict: The recognition of one's role in supporting an unjust system can lead to significant internal moral conflict. Individuals may struggle to reconcile their self-image with the reality of their actions or inactions that have contributed to broader societal harms.

Guilt and Shame: Feelings of guilt and shame can emerge as individuals grapple with the realization that they have been part of a system that oppresses others.

These emotions can be intensified by public criticism or personal confrontations with those who have suffered under the regime.

## Social and Familial Pressures

Pressure from Peer Groups: Social circles that continue to support the regime may exert pressure on individuals expressing doubt or guilt, potentially leading to social isolation for those questioning their complicity.

Generational Differences: Familial tensions may arise, particularly if younger family members hold more progressive views and challenge the older generation's support of or indifference to authoritarian practices.

## Crisis of Conscience and Psychological Impact

Existential Questions: Individuals may face existential questions about their purpose, values, and the kind of legacy they wish to leave. This can lead to a profound personal crisis, affecting mental health and daily functioning.

Cognitive Dissonance: The discomfort of cognitive dissonance, where one's actions conflict with their moral beliefs, can lead to stress, anxiety, and a reevaluation of personal and professional choices.

## Pathways to Redemption

Seeking Forgiveness and Making Amends: Some may seek ways to make amends for their complicity, such as publicly acknowledging their role, supporting victims of the regime, or using their resources to fight injustices.

Activism and Advocacy: Turning towards activism, individuals may channel their guilt and newfound awareness into constructive actions, advocating for policy changes, supporting human rights initiatives, or joining or forming opposition groups.

## Transformative Actions and Social Responsibility

Educational Efforts: Engaging in or funding educational programs that promote awareness of authoritarianism's impacts can help prevent future complicity by educating others.

Supporting Systemic Change: Beyond personal redemption, contributing to systemic change involves supporting efforts to restore democratic institutions, promote transparency, and ensure accountability in governance.

In Essence The journey from complicity in injustice to active resistance and ethical accountability is fraught with challenges but also opportunities for profound personal growth and societal contribution. For Privileged White Americans, confronting the ethical implications of their choices under an authoritarian regime can be a catalyst for transformative change, both personally and within the broader community. Recognizing their potential impact, they can play a pivotal role in dismantling oppressive structures and fostering a more just and equitable society.

# Legacy and Future Generations: The Long-Term Impact of Today's Decisions

The decisions and actions taken by the current generation, particularly under the influence of an authoritarian regime, can significantly shape the socio-political and economic landscape for future generations. As individuals navigate the complexities of governance, policy, and personal ethics, the legacy they leave behind can profoundly affect the freedom, prosperity, and unity of their descendants. This exploration delves into how today's choices might create long-lasting impacts that could lead to a less free, less prosperous, and more divided country, potentially burdening future generations with significant challenges and regrets.

### *Impact on Democratic Institutions*

Erosion of Democracy: Decisions that undermine democratic processes and institutions, such as curtailing free elections, limiting freedom of the press, or dismantling judicial independence, can lead to a weakened democratic framework. Future generations might inherit a political system where power is concentrated and democratic participation is stifled.

Difficulty in Reversing Authoritarianism: Once democratic institutions are eroded, restoring them can be exceedingly challenging. Future generations may struggle to reinstate these structures and may resent the choices that led to their weakening.

## Economic Legacy

Short-Term Gains vs. Long-Term Stability: Economic policies favoring immediate gain over sustainable growth. Significant tax cuts for the wealthy that deplete public resources or unchecked environmental exploitation can jeopardize long-term economic stability. Future generations might inherit an economy burdened with debt, depleted natural resources, and inadequate infrastructure.

Wealth and Opportunity Disparities: If current policies exacerbate wealth inequality, future generations could face heightened class divisions and reduced social mobility, leading to a society where opportunities are unevenly distributed.

## Social and Cultural Divides

Intensification of Divisions: Decisions that polarize societies, whether through discriminatory policies, divisive rhetoric, or neglect of minority rights, can deepen social and cultural rifts. The resultant fragmented society could be characterized by mistrust, resentment, and ongoing conflict among different groups.

Loss of Social Cohesion: As social bonds weaken due to increased polarization, the communal fabric essential for a united and cooperative society could be severely damaged, leaving a legacy of division and discord for future citizens.

## Global Standing and Relationships

Isolation on the World Stage: If the current generation's foreign policies lead to international isolation, future generations may find their country globally marginalized. This isolation can affect international trade, foreign investment, and political alliances, limiting the country's influence and prosperity.

Reputation and Influence: The reputation of a nation that turns toward authoritarianism can deter other nations from engaging in cultural, educational, or diplomatic exchanges. The country's perceived role as a global leader or partner might be significantly diminished, affecting how future generations are viewed and treated internationally.

## Responsibility to Future Generations

Consideration of Long-Term Impacts: Decision-makers and citizens alike must consider the long-term impacts of their actions on future generations. This involves prioritizing sustainable, equitable, and democratic practices that uphold the welfare and rights of all citizens.

Education and Legacy Building: Instilling values of democracy, sustainability, and social justice in younger generations can help mitigate negative legacies. Educational initiatives that promote critical thinking, civic engagement, and ethical leadership can empower future generations to address and rectify past mistakes.

## Strategies for Positive Change

Policy Reevaluation: Continuously reevaluating policies to ensure they align with long-term benefits rather than short-term gains is essential. This can help avoid decisions that future generations will regret.

Engagement and Dialogue: Fostering a culture of open dialogue and inclusive decision-making can help bridge divides and build a more unified society that future generations will inherit.

In Essence The legacy left by today's choices has the potential to shape the freedoms, prosperity, and social unity of future generations. By making decisions that prioritize the long-term health of democratic institutions, economic stability, and social cohesion, current generations can ensure that their descendants inherit a country that is not only free and prosperous but also characterized by a strong sense of community and fairness.

# Long-Term Impact of Authoritarian Shifts on Priviledge White Americans

The allure of short-term benefits from authoritarian policies can be compelling for some segments of the population, including Privileged White Americans. However, the erosion of democratic principles and the centralization of power can lead to profound long-term consequences. These effects extend beyond the immediate circle of influence, impacting freedoms, rights, and economic stability for the broader population, including those who might have initially supported or benefited from such changes.

## *Initial Support and Short-Term Benefits*

Economic Incentives: Initially, certain policies under authoritarian rule, such as tax cuts for the wealthy and deregulation, can create economic upturns that predominantly benefit the upper echelons of society, including many Privileged White Americans.

Enhanced Security Measures: Increased security measures and stringent law enforcement under authoritarian regimes can give a superficial sense of safety and order, appealing to those concerned about crime and stability.

## *Erosion of Democratic Safeguards*

Loss of Legal Protections: As the judiciary comes under the sway of authoritarian leaders, the rule of law can be compromised. This erosion affects all citizens' rights to fair legal proceedings, including those who initially supported the regime.

Suppression of Dissent: The curtailing of free speech and assembly rights can initially target specific groups but eventually expand to silence any opposition. This suppression stifles critical voices that are essential for a healthy democracy, including those within the privileged classes who may disagree with certain policies.

## *Economic Instability and Long-Term Risks*

Unsustainable Economic Policies: Short-term economic gains from deregulation and tax breaks often lead to longer-term economic problems, such as increased national debt, income inequality, and potential financial crises that can destabilize the entire economy.

Impact on Global Standing: The international isolation that can result from autocratic governance might lead to trade sanctions, reduced foreign investment, and lost business opportunities, affecting the economic interests of all national sectors.

## Social and Cultural Impacts

Increasing Social Divides: As wealth and power become more concentrated, social divides widen, leading to class resentment and social unrest. Privileged individuals might find themselves targets of public anger and frustration as the economic divide grows.

Cultural Stagnation: The lack of cultural exchange and the homogenization of thought under authoritarian regimes can lead to a decline in cultural richness and innovation, impacting everyone's quality of life, including the previously privileged.

## Threats to Personal Freedom and Security

Surveillance and Privacy Intrusions: Increased surveillance might initially target perceived threats but eventually extends to all citizens, including privileged groups, eroding privacy and personal freedoms.

Arbitrary Rule and Loss of Security: The unpredictability and capricious nature of authoritarian rule can lead to a general atmosphere of fear and insecurity, where no one, regardless of status, is immune from state caprices.

## Reevaluation and Potential for Change

Awareness and Pushback: The realization of these long-term risks might prompt reevaluation among those who initially supported authoritarian shifts.

This awareness can fuel movements for restoring democratic norms and governance.

Advocacy for Democratic Restoration: Engaging in or supporting advocacy efforts to restore democratic institutions and principles can help reverse some of the damages and ensure that future generations inherit a freer, more equitable society.

In Essence, While the shift toward authoritarianism might initially seem to benefit certain individuals, particularly Privileged White Americans, the broader, long-term effects can lead to a significant erosion of freedoms, economic stability, and social harmony. Recognizing the inherent risks and potential losses is crucial for any efforts aimed at preserving the democratic values that ensure a balanced and just society for all.

# Don't miss out!

Visit the website below and you can sign up to receive emails whenever Adrian Rocquecliffe publishes a new book. There's no charge and no obligation.

https://books2read.com/r/B-A-LUNRB-BMBYE

Did you love *The Republican Agenda: Undoing 200 Years of Democracy for a Dictatorship*? Then you should read *Making America Great Altogether - Call to Action*[1] by Adrian Rocquecliffe!

[2]

In our rallying cry, 'Making America Great Altogether – Call to Action,' unity takes center stage but with a twist. Instead of pushing for uniformity, we celebrate the vibrant patchwork of perspectives that make up our nation. It's about inclusivity, where every voice, no matter how different, is not just heard but cherished. This is not just a call. It's an invitation to be part of something bigger.

This call for unity recognizes that diversity isn't just a buzzword—it's the lifeblood of progress. By weaving together the varied threads of American society, we create a tapestry of resilience and innovation. Whether you're from a bustling city or a quiet country town, whether your roots trace back generations or you're a newcomer, your voice matters. You are an integral part of this collective progress.

---

1. https://books2read.com/u/mK25PP

2. https://books2read.com/u/mK25PP

But it's not just about warm fuzzies; it's practical, too. In a world where challenges come fast and furious, we need all hands on deck. By embracing our differences and fostering a culture of openness, we tap into a wellspring of creativity and insight that can steer us through even the toughest of times.

Let's ditch the divisiveness and roll out the welcome mat for all. In "Making America Great Altogether," we're not just talking the talk; we're walking the walk toward a future where everyone has a seat at the table.

Read more at https://www.makingamericagreataltogether.us/adrian_rocquecliffe.

# Also by Adrian Rocquecliffe

Making America Great Altogether - Call to Action
Trump's Vision of MAGA- The Fallacy
Extra! Extra! Read All About It
Trump's Insurrection of the US Capitol
How Well do you Know Your Candidate?
Trumpisms: Decoding the Rhetoric of Disruption
The Republican Agenda: Undoing 200 Years of Democracy for a Dictatorship
Under the Iron Flag: A Family's Battle for Survival and Justice in Trump's America
Complimentary Orchiectomy with First Sexual Offense: Starting at the Top
The Gulf of America: Trump's Vision for a United Continent
Project 2026 USA: We the People, For the People, By the People


Watch for more at https://www.makingamericagreataltogether.us/adrian_rocquecliffe.

# About the Author

Adrian Rocquecliffe's journey from a young boy navigating cultural divides to a successful entrepreneur and visionary leader exemplifies the American dream. His dedication to improving the country for future generations is a testament to his belief in the power of unity and collaboration. As he continues his work with "Making America Great Altogether," Adrian remains hopeful that his efforts will contribute to a better, more inclusive America when he retires.

Read more at https://www.makingamericagreataltogether.us/adrian_rocquecliffe.

# About the Publisher

Writers Sidekick Publishing is a key part of the Writers Sidekick Resource Hub. Writers Sidekick Publishing specializes in publishing anthologies that welcome submissions from both new and established authors, providing a platform to showcase their work and contribute to the literary world. Additionally, it produces exclusive books tailored to the needs of the Writers Sidekick Resource Hub community.